HOW TO HELP SOMEONE WITH POSTNATAL DEPRESSION

TRIGGER™

The mental health & wellbeing publisher

ABOUT THE AUTHOR

Dr Jenn Cooper is a chartered counselling psychologist with over ten years' experience working within adult mental health. Dr Jenn has developed a varied and dynamic portfolio career within healthcare settings, independent practice and academia.

A mother of two, Dr Jenn became especially interested in maternal mental health following her own mental health challenges after the arrival of her eldest daughter. From then, Dr Jenn has been committed to developing her practice and expertise to support women during their motherhood journey, from severe mental health difficulties to empowering mothers to rediscover their own identities.

Dr Jenn is committed to improving the wellbeing and mental health of people across the country, both in her independent practice and across her social media platforms.

Find out more at www.drjenncooper.com and on Instagram @mummy_matters__.

HOW TO HELP SOMEONE WITH POSTNATAL DEPRESSION

A Practical Handbook to Postpartum Depression and
Maternal Mental Health in the First Year

Dr Jenn Cooper

TRIGGER™
The mental health & wellbeing publisher

This edition published in 2023 by Trigger Publishing
An imprint of Shaw Callaghan Ltd

UK Office
The Stanley Building
7 Pancras Square
Kings Cross
London N1C 4AG

US Office
On Point Executive Center, Inc
3030 N Rocky Point Drive W
Suite 150
Tampa, FL 33607
www.triggerhub.org

A CIP catalogue record for this book is available upon request
from the British Library
ISBN: 978-1-83796-264-8
Ebook ISBN: 978-1-83796-265-5

Typeset by Lapiz Digital Services

To my beautiful daughters who inspire all that I do. Poppy and Imogen, my darling girls, you push me every day to be better and have shown me that to be the best mother to you girls, I need to look after my own wellbeing first.

Because of you I have found insight and passion in supporting and empowering mothers in their own journeys – so not only have you inspired and helped me, but you have a hand in the support I offer every mother I work with. You will never know the impact you have made on this world.

CONTENTS

INTRODUCTION

This book has been written for anyone who is supporting a loved one with postnatal/postpartum depression (PND/PPD). You are likely to be a partner, friend, parent or other family member of a new mum and may be unsure at this point whether she is experiencing the normal baby blues or perhaps something more. You may have noticed that she doesn't quite seem herself, or that she is finding the transition to motherhood more difficult than expected. Knowing what PND/PPD and other maternal mental health difficulties look like and being able to identify them is crucially important in helping your loved one to access the support she needs, when she needs it.

It is too much to expect a new mother to have the energy or insight to identify if something isn't quite right; for the most part she is probably just surviving hour by hour, day by day. By being equipped with the knowledge and insight to correctly identify the symptoms of PND/PPD, you can be her voice when she cannot voice it herself. You can be her advocate, when it is simply too difficult for her to advocate for herself. Understanding how your loved one is feeling and how you can help, without putting added pressure on her, will be hugely beneficial for her.

WHY I WROTE THIS BOOK

As a psychologist, I had worked therapeutically with a variety of maternal mental health difficulties. However, it was not until I had my eldest daughter that I could fully appreciate the impact of PND/PPD. I had naively assumed that, as a psychologist, I had all of the knowledge I needed and that PND/PPD would not affect me – and if it did, I would be well-equipped with the tools to get myself out of it. Unfortunately, maternal mental health difficulties do not discriminate, nor does professional insight protect you from them, and I spent a long first year of motherhood in the depths of PND/PPD.

I suspect my underlying assumptions about my supposed ability to cope exacerbated the expectations and self-criticism that I experienced during this time, and made it harder to acknowledge that I wasn't OK. I felt that I 'should' be able to deal with this, and so didn't speak up until my husband (who fortunately had some background in the medical field) raised the issue. I embarked on a journey to dismantling my own expectations and seeking support. And it helped. I felt better. I enjoyed motherhood more. And then I experienced PND/PPD again after my second daughter was born – because again, maternal mental health difficulties do not discriminate.

These experiences fuelled my interest and passion for understanding and working with maternal mental health difficulties. I wanted to support women to dismantle their own expectations of themselves and help them to enjoy motherhood in the way they so deserved. Since the birth of my second daughter, I have focused my career on building my expertise in maternal mental health, both working individually with mothers, but also educating and empowering those mothers who haven't yet been able to voice their struggles, and educating their loved ones.

In this book, I want to give you the tools to reach someone you know – a mother who hides in the shadow of her own assumptions and beliefs, as I did, so that she can be freed from them, and be allowed to heal and enjoy her life again (as I did).

WHO THIS BOOK IS FOR

While the majority of the information will be more relevant to a partner who is living with the person with PND/PPD, I recognize that you may also be a close relative or friend who is visiting or supporting from afar and, as such, have added particular sections and examples that may be more useful for you.

I want to be clear that your loved one does not need to have been formally diagnosed with PND/PPD for this book to be helpful for you. It might be a starting place for both of you, a way of talking about your concerns, especially if she is not aware that she is struggling and needs support.

You may be supporting someone with a newborn baby or a boisterous nine-month-old, or perhaps even an older baby or toddler. PND/PPD can affect women at any stage within the first year and, when it is left untreated, can often continue to be problematic long beyond this time frame.

ABOUT THIS BOOK

This book offers you an overview of PND/PPD, making you aware of the signs and symptoms. There is guidance on what your role is in your loved one's recovery, along with practical tools and strategies that you might be able to implement to alleviate some of her distress. There is also advice on accessing professional support, and what sort of options are available.

Watching and supporting someone struggling with PND/PPD can have a huge impact on your own wellbeing. So, importantly, this book also looks at how you, in your supporting role, can look after yourself.

MY APPROACH

In my professional practice, I implement an integrative approach, drawing upon a variety of therapeutic approaches including Person Centred Therapy (PCT), Cognitive Behavioural Therapy (CBT) and Compassion Focused Therapy (CFT), among others, to meet the individual needs of my clients. Being able to draw on a variety of approaches means clients can develop practical strategies for managing their difficulties using CBT, while also developing more kindness and compassion for themselves using CFT and PCT. Tailoring my approach to my clients is central to the work I do. In this book I draw upon all these approaches, and use a CBT approach in Chapter 7 to help you understand your loved one's thought processes. CBT is a collaborative, problem-focused talking therapy that has a wide evidence base for helping people manage difficulties such as anxiety and depression, including PND/PPD.

TERMINOLOGY

The terms used differ globally so both postnatal depression (PND) and postpartum depression (PPD) have been used throughout the book. Postnatal and postpartum refer to the period from birth up to one year. Prenatal relates to things that occur during pregnancy, and perinatal to things that occur during pregnancy and up to a year after the birth.

THE LIVED EXPERIENCE

Throughout the book you will find stories and experiences from mothers who have struggled with PND/PPD and those who have supported them. Many of these are from my Instagram community, who have generously offered their stories to bring the experience of PND/PPD to life. All names have been changed to maintain their anonymity.

Thank you for reading, and I truly hope the book helps both you and your loved one.

CHAPTER 1

WHAT IS POSTNATAL DEPRESSION?

Postnatal/postpartum depression (PND/PPD) is a type of depression that affects approximately one in ten of all new mothers following the birth of their baby. PND/PPD typically presents within the first four to six weeks following childbirth; however, the onset of symptoms can be seen any time within the first year following childbirth.

PND/PPD is a complex and frightening condition which can impact on a new mother's ability to function and bond with their baby, and affect their general wellbeing and mood. While PND/PPD has similar symptoms to general depression – low mood and difficulties in functioning – unlike general depression, the onset of symptoms of PND/PPD are specifically triggered following childbirth and often symptoms orientate around a woman's mothering/bond with their baby. It can leave new mothers and those supporting them feeling lost and helpless.

It is important to separate out what PND/PPD is and isn't, so that you know what is normal and when to access further support.

What PND/PPD is:

- Persistent feelings of overwhelm, sadness and guilt
- All-consuming
- Prolonged difficulties bonding with baby
- Increased and persistent anxiety/feelings of panic
- Feelings of hopelessness and worthlessness

What PND/PPD is not:

- The 'baby blues'
- 'Ordinary' depression
- 'Just' sleep deprivation
- 'Just' part of being a mother

The baby blues (see page 10) and the 'normal' challenges of caring for a newborn require additional TLC and support and will pass in time, while PND/PPD requires early intervention and specialist support to give a new mother the best (and quickest) chance of recovery and to allow her to enjoy motherhood.

In the midst of new motherhood, your loved one will not know the difference between the baby blues and PND/PPD, so by equipping yourself with this knowledge, you will be able to give her that objective perspective that might be lost to her.

"I didn't even know my daughter had PND/PPD until much later on when she told me. I just assumed she was being her usual over-anxious self and putting too many expectations on herself. I guess that was all part of it, but I wish I'd known more about PND/PPD at the time."
Lewis

ONSET OF PND/PPD

PND/PPD, while similar to general depression, is assessed using a specialist screening measure: the Edinburgh Postnatal Depression Scale. It may be diagnosed within one to two months after giving birth, but can manifest at any stage within the first year.

One of the difficulties with diagnosis is the fact that there is no defined 'danger point' of when it is most likely to appear. In the UK and US, women are typically screened during their six-week postnatal health check with their GP or OBGYN. A new mother will be asked about her mood, and may be screened for PND/PPD, but there is a misconception that if there is no sign of it at this check, it will not develop. If her mood deteriorates after this time, there is no other official screening point. As such, PND/PPD can be missed, and a new mother may struggle for many months before it is picked up, likely with the symptoms worsening over time.

When it is left untreated, the symptoms can continue to be problematic long beyond the first year. A woman may go on to be diagnosed with 'normal' depression, but the onset can be traced back to that first year following childbirth.

Additionally, while PND/PPD is defined as developing after giving birth, there is evidence that one-third of women actually experience symptoms of low mood during pregnancy. So, if your loved one has been experiencing prenatal low mood, then this puts her at a higher chance of going on to develop PND/PPD. (Note that not all women who experience prenatal low mood will go on to develop PND/PPD, but it is something to watch out for.)

CAUSES OF PND/PPD

PND/PPD is often associated with the hormonal changes that a woman experiences in pregnancy and childbirth. However, while these hormones certainly may have a part to play, they are unlikely to be the *cause*. All women go through hormonal changes during pregnancy and childbirth, but not all go on to develop PND/PPD. The causes are, unfortunately, much more complex and sometimes a lot less obvious.

Some of the factors that can make someone more vulnerable to PND/PPD include:

- Having a traumatic birth
- Being separated from the baby (for whatever reason)
- Grief
- Previous mental health difficulties
- Previous (or ongoing) abuse
- Difficulties with feeding the baby
- A poorly baby
- Medical complications
- Family/relationship difficulties
- Other stressful major life events

It has also been found that women who have experienced PND/PPD with other children are at a higher risk of developing PND/PPD again – between 30–70 percent more likely depending on the severity of symptoms.

HIGH EXPECTATIONS

Sometimes the reasons behind PND/PPD are much less obvious. Many women create a picture of what motherhood will look like, and how they will be as mothers. Unfortunately, the reality of motherhood is something that no one is fully prepared for. Often women's own expectations, either of how they will feel or how things will go, are not met. They can then become self-critical, believing they are not doing something right.

These expectations can also pave the way for disappointment, either in motherhood not quite being what was anticipated, or disappointment in themselves for 'not coping better'. It can also lead to confusion and worry when things don't go according to plan. When the baby doesn't eat or sleep, or when there isn't a feeling of overwhelming instant love for the baby, a new mother may fear there is something wrong, rather than these things being a normal part of motherhood.

On top of this, motherhood can leave women feeling totally out of control and, at times, utterly deskilled. Going from being an independent woman who was able to look after herself and manage her daily life to a woman who is responsible for meeting the needs of a new little person, without any training or knowledge, needing help, and not knowing the answers, can be such a dramatic shift in identity. A woman may go from feeling capable and competent to feeling utterly lost and unsure. Chronic sleep deprivation and little focus on her own self-care may mean she barely manages to get through the day, with nowhere near her usual levels of productivity and capacity. And then, to top it all, the mum guilt and self-criticism sets in, adding another layer of distress and pressure that makes motherhood a very challenging and, at times, painful transition.

Not every woman who experiences the above will go on to develop PND/PPD, but these fairly common experiences can make someone more vulnerable, particularly those women who have high expectations of themselves generally or who have been used to being in control of life and themselves. Having this stability taken away, while experiencing the pain of disappointment at unmet expectations, along with the hormonal and physical changes and the chronic sleep deprivation, can be a perfect storm for women to misinterpret themselves as a failure. It is this misinterpretation and self-blaming that can make a new mother vulnerable to PND/PPD and if there are other factors too (see Chapter 3), there can be an increased risk.

"While motherhood is always a huge transition, finding it hard to the point where it impacts on a woman's belief in herself is not always 'normal'."

So, although the causes of PND/PPD are not always straight-forward, being aware of some of the factors that might make your loved one more vulnerable will hopefully make it a little easier to spot. The key takeaway is that while motherhood is hard and is always a huge transition, finding it hard to the point where it impacts on a woman's belief in herself is not always 'normal'. And just because it's meant to be hard, does not mean that it is easy to cope with. Being alert to a mum struggling is really important, and not dismissing that struggle as a 'normal part of motherhood' is equally important.

KEY ASPECTS

We will delve into the symptoms of PND/PPD in more detail further on in this book; for now, let's have a quick glance at the key aspects of PND/PPD.

BONDING WITH BABY

One of the key aspects of PND/PPD will be your loved one's difficulties in bonding with her baby. This may be something that she expresses openly, or something that she tries to mask. She may feel that she doesn't know her baby, or feel that her baby doesn't like her. She may struggle to interact with her baby, outside of the necessary duties (which may also be a struggle), or she may simply want to avoid her baby all together. She may also show signs of the other extreme – of not wanting to ever leave her baby and be highly anxious.

LACK OF SELF-CARE

Your loved one may be struggling to look after herself and/or her baby and find even the most basic tasks – eating, hydrating, personal hygiene – challenging.

SLEEP ISSUES

Your loved one may start to struggle with her sleep – beyond the expected sleep disturbances caused by a newborn – from sleeping too much, to being surprisingly awake despite the sleep deprivation.

BEHAVIOURAL CHANGES

Other symptoms that you might notice include being more irritable or more anxious than usual, and having a sense of hopelessness or worthlessness. Your loved one may be afraid to be left alone with her baby or may become very anxious if the baby is not with her. She may begin to withdraw from you or others around her and might avoid seeing people or going out.

Typically, a mother struggling with PND/PPD will be experiencing a number of negative thoughts and feelings about herself and possibly about her baby. She may believe that she is not a good enough mother and that she is not coping; she may have low confidence and compare herself unfavourably to others; she may feel unnecessarily guilty about things. As such, she may not be able to find joy in anything – including her new baby.

She may suffer from anxiety and worry excessively about things, including her baby's health, weight, feeding etc., and perhaps the cleanliness or safety of her environment. She may even begin to worry that she might harm her baby, or that they are at some kind of risk. She may express thoughts of not loving her baby or may be struggling to bond with them.

In more severe cases, a mother with PND/PPD may express suicidal thoughts, engage in self-harm behaviours or experience psychotic symptoms – where she may hear voices or express unusual beliefs.

This has been a brief snapshot of the key aspects; keep in mind that PND/PPD is complicated and unique and how it presents will differ in every case.

> "She may begin to withdraw from you or others around her and might avoid seeing people or going out."

NOT THE BABY BLUES

PND/PPD is sometimes confused with 'the baby blues', but it is important to understand the difference between them.

The baby blues are associated with the *huge* hormonal and physical changes that occur in a woman's body in the days following childbirth, along with adapting to motherhood. Typically, around days three and four after the birth, women can experience intense emotions and mood swings. They may become very tearful, often reporting crying for no reason. They might become more irritable, and feel low or anxious. It is easy to see how the baby blues can get confused with

PND/PPD, as they share many of the same symptoms, but the baby blues is a normal reaction to the changes that occur after birth, and it usually eases off around day ten. While intense and very real, the baby blues are transient and pass in their own time. PND/PPD, on the other hand, is persistent and worsens over time. If a woman is experiencing mood disturbances beyond two weeks, we begin to consider that it might be PND/PPD rather than the baby blues.

However, while the baby blues are not the same as PND/PPD, they are very real and very distressing and can be the gateway to it, especially if there are other factors that impact on a woman's mental health. Therefore, it can be helpful to have some strategies to help a mum through these difficult days.

"While the baby blues are not the same as PND/PPD, they are very real and very distressing and can be the gateway to it."

HOW TO HELP

Here are some suggestions for helping your loved one through the baby blues:

- Remember that she is recovering from a huge physical ordeal. While she may look like she's coping, her body has been through a huge amount and it takes time to recover. Encourage her to stay in bed. Remind her to take breaks and rest, even if she's hell-bent on 'getting back to normal'.

- Make life easy for her – pick up the extra load. Do the washing, make the meals, clean the toilet. Do what you can to lighten her load and allow her to ride the emotional waves of new motherhood.

- When the emotions come, let them be. Hold her, be the shoulder to cry on, grab the tissues. These are not emotions that you need to 'fix'; they are normal and necessary. While it can be distressing to see your loved one feeling overwhelmed, tired and upset, unless she is asking you to solve a problem, just be with her. Acknowledge the feelings, acknowledge that they are hard, acknowledge that this is all hard; ask what you can do, but most of all just be present with her.

- If you find your loved one is being snappy or more irritable than usual, as hard as it is, try not to take it personally. When we are tired and emotional, we tend to take those feelings out on those we feel the safest with, and that will probably mean you bear the brunt. But remind yourself that she has been through a huge ordeal, and that these feelings are temporary. Instead of getting defensive (which is a totally natural response), take a deep breath, ask if there is anything she needs, make her a cup of tea and tell her that you can help with whatever she needs.

- If you are a partner struggling to reassure and comfort your loved one, call in the troops – perhaps her mother, sister or friends. She may not want to see people, but having a close family member or friend pop over can give her someone else to offload to, and offer some support.
- Know that the baby blues will pass and try not to panic. Keep offering support and love.
- If you are a partner, it can be difficult if all the attention is on the mother. Remember that your wellbeing matters too. Make sure you are looking after yourself as best as you can and if you need to, find someone you can talk it all through with. Don't forget about your own emotions in all of this.
- If the baby blues persist beyond two weeks following the birth, seek additional support. Speak to the health visitor or give your family doctor a call. They will be able to point you in the right direction of accessing additional support, and will be able to arrange an assessment.

"At a baby massage class about six weeks in, I asked about the baby blues and the other women's experience of it was so different to mine. They laughed about crying

into their dinner for a few days – and I remember thinking, you only cried into your dinner? And you aren't feeling that way now? I suspected something more might be up for me."

Melanie

OTHER MATERNAL MENTAL HEALTH DIFFICULTIES

This section is designed to give you a brief overview of other mental health difficulties that might occur in new mothers. If you have concerns that your loved one is exhibiting any of the symptoms outlined here, seek advice from a healthcare professional.

POSTNATAL ANXIETY

Similar to PND/PPD, but not as well known, postnatal anxiety develops within the first year following childbirth but can also begin in pregnancy. It is very common for women to experience anxiety and depression at the same time, but it is possible for one to exist without the other. Symptoms include:

- Excessive worrying
- Finding it difficult to relax
- Constantly imagining the worst-case scenario

- Feeling that you have little to no control over the worrying
- Reassurance-seeking
- Dissociation (detachment from reality/zoning out)
- There may also be a variety of physical sensations including a fast heartbeat, palpitations, feeling sick, sweating, breathing faster or feeling that it is hard to breathe, feeling hot, being dizzy, having butterflies in the stomach.

You may notice your loved one experiencing panic attacks or anxiety episodes. She may also become fearful of certain places and people, and may start to avoid going out or doing things. It is easy to see how postnatal anxiety can be confused with PND/PPD, as many of the symptoms overlap, but the main difference in postnatal anxiety is that the focus is on the worry; in PND/PPD, there will be low mood.

PERINATAL OBSESSIVE-COMPULSIVE DISORDER (OCD)

Perinatal OCD is an anxiety disorder that affects approximately two to three women in every 100 in pregnancy and up to a year following childbirth. It is characterized by persistent, intrusive, anxiety-provoking thoughts or images (obsessions), and thoughts, actions or behaviours that are repeated in order to reduce the anxiety (compulsions). The types of obsessions experienced by women suffering from perinatal OCD might include:

- Thoughts about hurting the baby, both physically and sexually (having these thoughts is no indication of actually harming the baby)
- Preoccupation with germs or cleanliness
- Worries and doubts about having done or not done something (e.g. sterilizing the bottle properly)
- Believing that they need to get everything 'perfect'

Some of the behaviours (compulsions) you might notice your loved one exhibiting include:

- Rituals around excessive washing, cleaning, sterilizing
- Avoiding 'contamination' by not allowing others to hold the baby
- Seeking reassurance that she hasn't hurt the baby
- Avoiding changing the baby in case she hurts or touches the baby inappropriately or avoiding being left alone with the baby
- Constantly checking that the baby is OK
- Repeating obsessional thoughts – e.g. counting or praying to stop 'bad things from happening'

Perinatal OCD is quite markedly different from PND/PPD, with a focus on the irrational and unfounded worries about harming the baby and resultant behaviours. This is a very distressing disorder for women, as they are unable to tell the difference between a worry and a real threat. If you believe that your loved one might be suffering from perinatal OCD, speak with your healthcare provider as soon as possible.

POSTNATAL POST-TRAUMATIC STRESS DISORDER (PTSD) AND BIRTH TRAUMA

Postnatal PTSD and Birth Trauma are mental health conditions triggered by traumatic and/or life-threatening experiences during childbirth. Experiences that can trigger Birth Trauma include:

- Going through a very difficult, painful and long labour
- An emergency during labour, where the safety of the mother and/or the baby were at risk
- An unplanned Caesarean section
- Other emergency treatments and invasive interventions during labour
- Other very distressing, unexpected and traumatizing experiences during labour

Often people dismiss these experiences by claiming that 'all labours are traumatic' or by undermining the emotional experience if everyone is 'OK in the end'. This gives the mother the message that because everyone is safe, it no longer matters. This could not be further from the truth, and the act of dismissing these emotional and traumatic experiences can exacerbate this mental health condition further. The impact of PTSD or Birth Trauma can be long-lasting and affect the relationship between a mother and her baby. It can leave a mother feeling like a 'failure' or even feel a sense of grief at the positive labour experience she lost.

"It is important not to dismiss a woman's experience of a birth being traumatic, even if the events do not seem objectively traumatic."

Symptoms tend to fall into three different categories:

Re-experiencing: The mother might experience intrusive memories or flashbacks of the traumatic birth; she may feel as though she is actually there or may experience nightmares related to the events.

Hypervigilance: The mother may be hyper-alert, jumpy, panicky, restless and on edge. She may be looking for danger everywhere and react to non-threatening situations with real fear.

Avoidance: The mother might begin to avoid thinking or talking about her labour experience, including avoiding reminders of it. She may use avoidance strategies, including keeping very busy and using alcohol or drugs. By detaching from her emotions she might also detach from her baby and loved ones. She may also experience gaps in her memory of the event, where her brain represses the frightening and distressing parts of the experience.

As well as having a significant impact on a mother's emotional wellbeing, Birth Trauma can lead to PND/PPD and other mental health conditions, interfere with her ability to bond with the baby, and lead to anxiety about future pregnancies. It is important not to dismiss a traumatic birth as 'normal' and it is important not to dismiss a woman's experience of a birth being traumatic, even if the events do not seem objectively traumatic. It is a woman's subjective experience that matters the most in this instance, so take time to talk through her experience, listening out for the symptoms highlighted above. Acknowledge that the experience sounds traumatic and offer support. This might be in encouraging her to talk through it, or it may be helping her to access additional support. Most importantly, identifying this condition early will help to offset any further mental health difficulties (including PND/PPD) further down the line.

> "I experienced Birth Trauma and PTSD, which were missed and evolved into PND/PPD."
> Michelle

POSTPARTUM PSYCHOSIS

Postpartum psychosis is a serious mental health condition experienced by approximately 1 in 1,000 women, thankfully making it quite rare. If you believe that your loved one is experiencing symptoms of postpartum psychosis, it is essential to seek help immediately. Symptoms tend to have a rapid onset within a few weeks after childbirth and include psychosis, depression and mania.

- There may be rapid and unpredictable mood swings, going from feeling excited or elated to severely depressed.
- The woman may become confused and disorientated, and experience delusions (strong, irrational beliefs) or hallucinations (experiencing things that aren't there). She may report hearing voices or believing that she is being followed or having her mind read.

The symptoms of postpartum psychosis tend to be extreme and unusual and very out of character for the individual. It is imperative that women experiencing these kinds of symptoms are assessed and treated early. They may not agree that there is a problem and may resist help, but it is important to seek support straight away, regardless of their wishes.

WHEN DOES PND/PPD 'GET BETTER'?

Early intervention is key to recovery. If left untreated, PND/PPD can spill over into a woman's life beyond those early months of motherhood leading to more general depression, but the good news is that it is very treatable. Some women will begin to feel better on their own, without treatment, within three to six months; while for those who have access to support and treatment, symptoms can begin to subside within three or four months. Being able to identify PND/PPD early on and begin to implement the right support for your loved one will help.

"I truly felt like it was never-ending, but then I noticed a few months after starting therapy that the days felt a little easier and I was smiling a little more. I didn't believe that I could feel better during those really dark days, but I did."
Lucia

KEY POINTS TO REMEMBER

- PND/PPD is a type of depression which affects mothers, often presenting in the first four to six weeks following childbirth and is usually screened for at the six-week postnatal/postpartum check; however, symptoms can manifest at any time in the first postpartum year.
- Hormonal changes are associated with the onset of PND/PPD; however, there are many complex factors that make women vulnerable to PND/PPD – including pre-existing mental health difficulties, Birth Trauma, medical

complications, relationship difficulties and separation from baby.

- Women who have experienced PND/PPD with previous babies are more at risk of developing PND/PPD with subsequent children.
- Adjustment to motherhood can be challenging, and high expectations and less control over life can contribute to developing PND/PPD.
- Key features of PND/PPD include: poor self care, disrupted sleep (beyond what is normal with a baby), difficulties bonding with baby and meeting baby's needs, psychological changes including irritability, anxiety, negative beliefs, and feelings of worthlessness and hopelessness.
- In severe cases, PND/PPD can lead to suicidal thoughts, self-harm behaviours and/or psychotic symptoms. If your loved one experiences any of these, you should seek out help immediately from your healthcare provider or emergency services.
- PND/PPD is not 'general depression', as its onset is specifically related to having a child, even though symptoms can look similar.
- PND/PPD goes beyond the 'baby blues'.

- Other mental health conditions that can be experienced by new mothers, with or without PND/PPD, include postnatal anxiety, Perinatal OCD, Birth Trauma and Postnatal PTSD, Postpartum Psychosis.
- Recovery from PND/PPD varies, however, early intervention and support is essential.

Now that we have a clearer sense of what PND/PPD is and isn't, and an understanding of some of the background causes and related difficulties, let's move on to consider what the experience of PND/PPD might look like for your loved one.

CHAPTER 2

WHAT PND/PPD LOOKS LIKE

Now that we have a good understanding of what postnatal/postpartum depression is, let's break down what it might look like for your loved one. It is important to recognize that depending on your relationship with the person you are helping, you may see more or less of the symptoms outlined in this chapter. As her partner, you are likely to see more of the difficulties she is experiencing; as a friend, you may not have as much opportunity to see her and how she is truly feeling; if you are an involved family member, who visits often, you will likely be somewhere in the middle. You can only go on what you notice when you are around the person, but hopefully by knowing what to look out for you will be able to look beyond the snapshots you get of her.

A useful way to gain an insight into how your loved one might be feeling is by looking at their behaviour and the way they are expressing their thoughts. This approach is derived from the

CBT model of therapy that I touched upon in the introduction and will unpack in more detail in Chapter 7. This model suggests that our thoughts and behaviour impact directly on how we feel physically and emotionally, and that to make changes to our emotions and physical sensations, we must change the way we think and behave.

Unfortunately, we cannot mind read and so can't easily identify exactly how someone is feeling, either emotionally or physically! However, by looking out for changes in their behaviour or thinking, we can gain some clues as to what might be going on for them internally.

A 'NORMAL' PART OF MOTHERHOOD?

Your loved one might not recognize that there is a problem. She might think that her low mood, intrusive thoughts and difficulties in coping are a 'normal' part of motherhood. Or she might be so lost in her negative thoughts that she cannot see another possible explanation for how she feels, other than her being a terrible mother. Remember, we trust our thoughts. We are not in a habit of questioning them, and so when we are feeling overwhelmed, low, sleep deprived and struggling, thoughts of inadequacy and 'not-enoughness' are easy to believe.

"Being able to recognize the negative thoughts and behaviours will help you to identify when your loved one needs some extra support."

So it is your job in your supporting role to notice when some of these thoughts and behaviours might not simply be 'normal' motherhood, or when they do not match up with your own knowledge of your loved one's 'enoughness' as a mother. Being able to recognize the negative thoughts and behaviours will help you to identify when your loved one needs some extra support. Do look out for some of the physical and emotional symptoms too. You might be able to help your loved one name her feelings by talking things through with her.

BEHAVIOUR IN PND/PPD

If I asked you to tell me what you thought PND/PPD looks like, you might describe it as:

- 'Mum crying all the time.'
- 'Mum being sad.'
- 'Not bonding with baby.'

But actually, PND/PPD has a whole host of symptoms, and it will be different for every mother; it may even be different for the same person with different children. So this chapter is not designed to give you a comprehensive list of behaviours that will identify PND/PPD, but an insight into the sort of things to look out for. I have broken these behaviours down into different categories; someone doesn't have to exhibit behaviours from all categories to be suffering from PND/PPD.

CHANGES IN THE MOTHER

Some of the behavioural symptoms can be difficult to differentiate from the normal impact of having a baby. Things like sleep disturbance, fatigue, lack of routine, and being more emotional can be part and parcel of adapting to having a little person interrupt every aspect of life. It is when there are more prolonged and persistent changes that we might consider that these 'normal' behaviours are indicative of PND/PPD.

You may begin to notice changes in your loved one's behaviour, including her sleep, eating and energy levels. You might notice she is sleeping more than usual, not wanting to get out of bed, or indeed the opposite – that she refuses to, or cannot sleep, even when she has the opportunity to do so. This is particularly challenging to identify, given that sleep disturbance is central to motherhood. However, if your loved one is struggling to get out of bed, or finding it very difficult to sleep when she has the opportunity, then we would consider that this might be a behavioural symptom of PND/PPD. Similarly, extreme fatigue might be an indicator of PND/PPD. Again, it is difficult to differentiate from the expected fatigue, but if your loved one appears to be exceptionally lethargic, lacking in motivation and low in energy, this may be a warning sign of PND/PPD. You may also notice an increase in energy that might appear out of character, and not fitting with the amount of rest or sleep that your loved one is getting.

Similarly, finding time to eat, or indeed even remembering to eat with a baby can be a challenge, but a mother with PND/PPD may have difficulty eating, even when she is provided with the opportunity and a meal is put in front of her. Or the opposite might be true: she might be overeating, but again this is difficult to identify, especially in breastfeeding mums, where an increased appetite is normal. Again, this is where you, as her loved one, will know best – is her eating significantly different from usual? Even when you encourage her, is she refusing or disinterested? Is she eating significantly more than is normal? Remember that you know your loved one, and even with all the changes that motherhood brings, you will be an excellent judge of what is normal for her.

You may notice that your loved one is struggling to maintain a daily routine, and it is impacting her basic self-care, such as showering or even brushing her teeth. She may have no interest in maintaining any of her usual routines, including sleeping and eating as we discussed above.

"I would become irritated without any provocation. I felt like my behaviour was really irrational, but I couldn't control it."
Louisa

You may also notice that her personality has changed somewhat. She may be more irritable and snappy, having little to no tolerance of others or to things going wrong. Or indeed, she may be withdrawn and quiet, struggling to engage in conversation with others, and keeping to herself more than usual.

Putting On a Brave Face

Your loved one may put on a 'brave face', due to the guilt and perceived stigma attached to feeling anything other than blissfully happy when she's had a baby. She may not, on the face of it, appear to be behaving that differently and may insist that she is 'fine'. This, of course, may be true and is what we would hope for, but be mindful that she may feel unable to voice how she is feeling. Look out for subtle changes in personality, such as being more passive and putting up with things or people that she usually wouldn't. Again, your experience of your loved one will speak volumes – if something feels a bit off, ask her how she is really doing; give her explicit permission to perhaps not be coping quite as well as she might be showing.

"Look out for subtle changes in personality, such as being more passive and putting up with things or people that she usually wouldn't."

Emotional Rollercoaster

It is common for someone with PND/PPD to exhibit a range of emotional symptoms including crying more than usual; getting easily and quickly frustrated; swinging from being OK to frustrated, to bursting into tears. Your loved one may appear to gain little to no enjoyment out of anything, or certainly less enjoyment in the things she usually would. She may appear detached and disinterested, whether that be in others, the baby or herself. Alternatively, you might notice she appears apathetic and perhaps a bit numb. She may not be displaying any kind of emotion, not getting annoyed at things she might usually find frustrating and appearing to have 'checked out' of situations.

"Everything had to be done my way or else I grew frustrated and my partner and I would start bickering, which made me feel worse. I was never like that before the PND/PPD."
Connie

"I would go from rage to exhaustion, to anger and to tears ... just so many tears."
Jessica

Or there may be an increase in anxious behaviours. Your loved one might behave in an overly controlling manner, seeking control over everything or refusing to let others help. She may be doing things that don't really need doing, like excessive cleaning or tidying.

BEHAVIOUR WITH THE BABY

Often PND/PPD can impact the relationship or bond a mother has with her baby, and while there isn't necessarily a 'normal' way of being, there are some warning signs to look out for, which can be broken down loosely into two categories: preoccupation and avoidance. However, bear in mind that while these behaviours are important to look out for, a woman does not need to be at either end of the extremes to be experiencing PND/PPD.

Preoccupation

You may notice your loved one becoming overly preoccupied with her baby, rarely putting him or her down. This should not be confused with a mother cuddling her baby. You cannot cuddle your baby too much – contrary to the old wives' tales of 'creating a rod for your own back' should you let the baby fall asleep in your arms. It is normal for a new mother to be obsessed with her newborn – not only because they are entirely squishable, but also because it is a primitive drive to protect. However, when a mum won't put her baby down or seems very reluctant to pass the baby on to someone else, it might be an indication of preoccupation. She may put off eating, sleeping or going to the toilet due to fears of putting the baby down. She may struggle to attend to the needs of other children due to being unable to separate herself from her baby. This level of anxious preoccupation may be indicative of someone who is really struggling with the idea of not having her baby close. And while on some level this is normal, a mum should feel able and safe enough to go for a shower or a pee!

You may also notice that your loved one is continually checking on the baby, both through the day and during the night. During the day, she might refuse to put the baby down, or constantly check the baby's temperature and nappies, or Google every little noise or movement the baby makes. She may also obsess over how much the baby is feeding and sleeping. Again, this can be normal behaviour, especially for breastfeeding mothers who can struggle to gauge how much milk their baby is getting, but if the obsession begins to interfere with the mother's wellbeing or mood, then it is perhaps out of the realms of 'normal'.

"You may notice that your loved one is continually checking on the baby, both through the day and during the night."

You might also find that your loved one is staying awake at night or waking herself up to check on her baby, without any obvious reason to do so. She may insist on doing everything herself and refuse to allow others to help. She may refuse the opportunity to sleep or eat or shower, feeling that she must be with her baby at all times. These kinds of behaviours are fairly normal in the early days – again due to this primal need for proximity and closeness to our infants, but it usually dissipates as our brains acclimatize and we feel that we and our baby are safe in our environment. So, if this kind of behaviour persists beyond those early days, it is possible that your loved one is struggling to trust that things feel safe enough for her to even stray to the bathroom without her baby.

"I experienced crippling anxiety and lack of belief in myself that I could keep my baby alive when I was suffering with PND/PPD."
Erica

Avoidance

At the other end of the spectrum is a mother who avoids her baby. She might avoid being alone with the baby or avoid attending to the baby's needs. This may be very noticeable, or it could be subtle. For example, she might suddenly 'need to do something' whenever the baby is due to be fed, or she might often pass the baby to others to hold, framing this as 'cuddles'. Or she may actively voice that she does not want to hold or look after the baby, especially if she is left on her own. Other avoidance behaviours to look out for are detachment behaviours. So even when she is looking after her baby, she may avoid looking at and engaging with the baby, attending only to his or her basic needs.

"I remember having a sense of panic every time my husband said he was going out, I think that's when the PND/PPD started. I'd offer to go, or suggest we ask someone else to pick up the milk. I couldn't bear the idea of being left alone with my baby. Not because I thought I'd do anything wrong, but mostly because I simply didn't know what to do. I was expressing at the time and felt more like a milk cow than a mother and I can vividly remember sitting there with the breast pump on, staring at this baby and feeling utterly numb. I wasn't sad really, just detached. As if she were there, but not really there. When my husband walked through the door I'd hand her straight to him. He seemed to find it so easy and I just couldn't work out why I found it so hard. I felt ashamed and like I just didn't have the 'mum-gene' in me."
Kate

BEHAVIOUR WITH OTHERS

You might notice that your loved one behaves differently with you or other people. She may be more withdrawn, avoiding speaking to or seeing people. Again, these behaviours range from very obvious to more subtle, and how much you notice will likely depend on your relationship with your loved one and how much time you spend with her. She may openly voice that she doesn't want to speak to or see anyone, or you may notice that she comes up with reasons to avoid others – for example, she might go for a nap or urgently need to do something when people are due to visit. She may cancel on people at the last minute or may refuse from the outset to make plans. You might notice that when others are around, she is quieter than usual; that she avoids the conversation or is minimal in her responses. She may avoid discussing how she is feeling or may gloss over this.

"It is especially helpful for you to be aware of these behaviours so that you can be her voice if she struggles to speak up."

Remember, a mother struggling with PND/PPD very often does not feel able to voice her experience and may attempt to put a 'brave face' on in front of others. You might therefore notice that she changes her behaviour around others to avoid talking about it.

This might be particularly true with any healthcare professionals. It is especially helpful for you to be aware of these behaviours so that you can be her voice if she struggles to speak up.

Alternatively, you may find that your loved one is desperate to have others around, especially if she wants to avoid being left alone with her baby. Of course, it is normal for a new mother to want and indeed need help after having a baby, but if she is scared of being alone, and is allowing others to take over from her, this is perhaps something to explore with her.

> "After having my baby, my friends would check in on me and ask how I was doing. I couldn't bring myself to say anything more than 'fine'. They started to get more worried about me and so I just completely withdrew from them. It was easier to avoid the questions than to have to make up an answer."
>
> Elspeth

THINKING PROBLEMS

In many ways, identifying and spotting some of the behaviours present in PND/PPD is much easier than identifying some of the thoughts. It is that difference between what is observable and what is not. Rather than teaching you how to mind read (unfortunately an impossible task!), I want to give you an insight into the internal thoughts that might be going on for your loved one and give you some clues to the kind of statements to listen out for.

'I'M NOT DOING THIS RIGHT'

She might be feeling that she isn't cut out for this whole motherhood thing. She likely had a picture in her head about what motherhood would look like, and if it is not living up to that ideal (which it rarely does anyway), she is very likely to blame herself. A good example is when the baby is crying and is not easily settled she thinks that *she* is the problem – she cannot soothe her baby, therefore *she* must be doing something wrong.

> "I remember having a physical reaction every time my baby cried. It was a surge of panic and I'd start thinking what I'd gotten wrong. I remember even telling my mother that the baby shouldn't need to cry if I was meeting her needs correctly. So, every time she did cry I would start beating myself up and telling myself that I was doing something wrong and that I was a terrible mum. I couldn't see another possible reason for her crying if it wasn't because I was doing something wrong. Looking back now, I can see just how unwell I was – babies cry regardless of what you do!"
>
> Jen

Now, most of us know that sometimes babies just cry, and sometimes they are not easily soothed, which is anxiety provoking and distressing (after all, a baby's cries literally send us into threat mode). However, most of us can rationalize that sometimes there is nothing we can do, and that it is unlikely that we are doing something wrong. A mother struggling with PND/PPD will think quite differently. She might take it personally ('My baby hates me') or she might assume she is failing ('What kind of mother am I if I can't even soothe my baby?'). She might become fixated on these beliefs and be unable to see any other perspectives. With this can come a sense of worthlessness, and a loss of confidence in any aspect of her being – 'If I can't do this, what can I do right?'

These kinds of thoughts can lead to 'I can't do this'. A mother struggling with PND/PPD may be feeling trapped, inadequate and perhaps even believe that she is a danger to her baby, or that her baby is better off without her. She may avoid doing certain things or give up easily when things aren't going well. She may openly tell you that she can't do it, and while you know that she can, she will not be easily reassured. She may even begin to think about running away, believing that her baby would at the very least be fine without her, and likely better off.

What to Look Out For

You may notice that your loved one lacks confidence, getting easily frustrated or overwhelmed when she's struggling. It might be that she gives herself a really hard time for getting something 'wrong', or she may be questioning why she's struggling. She may ask you to take over because you are 'better at it'; or she might get easily offended if you offer to help, perhaps feeling that this is an indication that you don't think she can do it. It is normal for any new parent to question and worry about whether they are getting things right, but most new parents can be fairly easily reassured that they are doing just fine. A mother with PND/PPD is unlikely to be reassured, no matter how often she is told.

"When the baby is crying and is not easily settled, the mother thinks that *she* is the problem."

'I'M A TERRIBLE MUM'

Your loved one is likely to be self-critical and unfairly judge herself *a lot*. She will have had an idea of what kind of mother she wanted to be and, in not living up to that ideal, self-blame can become a real problem. She is likely to feel guilty about *everything* – from not being able to soothe her baby to not being cut out for motherhood; or simply feeling guilty for not enjoying looking after her baby. This guilt leads to an assumption that she has something to feel guilty about and she will begin to attribute meaning to these feelings – 'I'm a terrible mum'; 'I'm letting my baby down'; 'I'm damaging my baby'.

"She might believe that everyone around her is managing so much better than she is."

Have you ever heard the saying 'comparison is the thief of joy'? Well, for a mother struggling with PND/PPD this is likely to be a daily occurrence. As she already believes that she is a terrible mother, she will look at those around her and wonder why it is that they have got it all together. She might sit with friends or at a baby group (if she manages to get out of the door) and believe that everyone around her is managing so much better than she is. She will believe that all these other mothers are 'naturals' or simply more competent than her. She will believe that she is the odd one out, and that everyone is so much better than she is. She may also begin to question what is so different about her, which can cycle back round to her believing that she simply isn't cut out for the role.

"I didn't believe that I deserved to be a mum. I thought my baby deserved better than me."
Polly

What to Look Out For

A mother stuck in this cycle might tell you that everyone would be better off without her. She might tell you that everyone else is doing things so much better than her, and might voice words like 'failure' or 'not good enough'. She might be focusing on only the things that are difficult or that have gone wrong, and be ignoring anything that she is doing well. She will, again, find it difficult to be reassured despite your best efforts.

You might also notice that she tries to live up to what other people are doing. She might hear that someone is doing sleep training and believe that she should also be doing sleep training, even if that goes against what she wants to do. She might be easily led by others because she assumes everyone knows better than she does.

'WHY DON'T I LOVE MY BABY?'

One of the common symptoms of PND/PPD is around having difficulties bonding with the baby. This can be for a number of reasons, either from Birth Trauma (see page 17), exhaustion or simply that bonding isn't always that easy. However, women with PND/PPD can experience these difficulties for much longer. It might begin with worrying about not experiencing that sudden rush of pure, unadulterated love when that little being is placed in their arms, and may grow into a complete detachment from the baby.

"She may assume that she is doing something wrong if she does not feel the love she expected to feel."

A mother struggling with PND/PPD might look at her baby and wonder why she cannot love it. She may question whether what she feels is normal or enough, and is likely to assume that she is doing something wrong if she does not feel the love she expected to feel. She may beat herself up for this and use it as evidence of her being a terrible mother, or she may even look at it with detached confusion. She may be plagued with thoughts of desperately wanting to love her baby, or not. She might simply be resigned to the fact that there is something inherently wrong with her, making her incapable of this love.

"I just felt numb. I couldn't understand why I didn't have that sudden rush of love. I just felt empty and hated myself for not loving my baby. As time went on, and I still hadn't gotten that rush, I really thought I'd never feel it – it was actually quite scary."
Pauline

"It [PND/PPD] was like an all-encompassing sense of failure at something that I felt should be so easy – who doesn't love their baby?"
Erica

What to Look Out For

- A mother struggling to bond with her baby might appear rather disinterested in her baby or she might constantly question what is wrong with her.
- She might be looking at other people around her and wonder why they find it so easy when she is finding it impossible.
- Again, you might hear her blame and criticize herself for everything.
- She might question why things haven't panned out the way she had expected and worry about the future.
- You might notice that she makes comments about things never getting better or conveys a sense of hopelessness.

'WHAT IF … ?'

A mother struggling with PND/PPD might be plagued with anxiety and be consumed with 'What ifs …' and struggle to reassure herself that things are OK. This constant worry and rumination can lead to her questioning the safety of herself, others and the world around her. A woman who previously was outgoing and independent suddenly begins to panic at the idea of leaving the house or seeing people. She might worry that something bad will happen or that someone might discover that she's not coping. The worries can be far reaching, both about herself and her baby. She might become fixated on 'danger' and on getting things 'right'.

What to Look Out For

- A mother suffering from anxiety and PND/PPD might become fixated on certain things – e.g. the cleanliness of the baby's bottles, or the safety of things in and outside the home.
- She may become over-anxious about the baby's wellbeing or may be convinced that something terrible is about to happen.
- She might voice these concerns, or she might withhold them, but adapt her behaviour as described previously.
- She may not be able to let go of the worries that she experiences, some of which may not be something you would deem as of any concern.

'I WISH ... '

A woman struggling with PND/PPD may also begin to experience regrets or resentment. She may wish that she had never fallen pregnant or begin to feel resentful toward others and/or her baby. Given the weight of the pain and distress she is experiencing, these regrets and resentment are understandable. However, she may feel horrified for having these thoughts in the first place, or she may entirely believe them.

She may beat herself up for thinking this way or she might become fixated on a time when life was different. It can be here that thoughts of needing to escape can appear. She may exhibit beliefs that everyone would be fine without her, and fantasies of a life free of responsibility and pain. These regrets and resentment are understandable, but not necessarily how she really feels. More likely, these are a reaction to the enormous stress and pressure she is under, but a mother struggling with PND/PPD is unlikely to be able to separate herself out from that. She will likely use this as evidence of her being a horrible mother, which again fuels this vicious cycle.

> "I had all these horrible thoughts of 'What have I done?' and 'I can't go back on this now'."
> Polly

> "I kept thinking – I've had a baby, but I'm not sure I should have done as the changes felt too massive."
> Amaya

What to Look Out For

- Your loved one may voice her thoughts around regret and resentment or she may seek reassurance that she has done the right thing in having a baby.
- She may begin to talk about all the things she's not able to do and may voice frustration at this.
- She may begin to make plans for the future where her role as a mother is less prominent.

- She may look at finding ways to avoid the responsibilities of motherhood and may begin to act more recklessly than usual.

SUICIDAL THOUGHTS

A mother experiencing severe PND/PPD may begin to think about ending her own life. These may be thoughts along the lines of 'I hope I don't wake up in the morning', or 'I'd be better off dead'. She may experience these as a passing thought, or she may begin to engage with these thoughts and begin to formulate a plan in her head. She may believe that she is utterly worthless and that the future is bleak. She will believe that everyone would be better off without her and may not be able to find a reason to stay alive.

What to Look Out For

- Thoughts around being better off dead, or that others would be better off without her are red flags. This is very distressing to hear and likely very upsetting. If your loved one begins to express thoughts like this, it is important to act quickly and engage with your healthcare provider, or call emergency services.
- Less obviously, noticing comments about worthlessness or apathy about the future might indicate that a mother is struggling with suicidal thoughts.

- Hopelessness is also a warning sign, and so if mum is voicing that she doesn't believe things can get better, this might be something to follow up on.

CONSIDER THE WHOLE PICTURE

The thoughts and behaviours that accompany PND/PPD often co-exist and interweave with each other. Separating them out is almost misleading, as often the thoughts trigger the behaviours, and the behaviours give us insight into the thoughts. So being aware of all aspects of your loved one's experience is very useful. Be on the lookout for the whole package, rather than individual symptoms. And again, be mindful that some of the symptoms are a normal part of motherhood, but it is the frequency, intensity and relentlessness of the symptoms that define PND/PPD.

KEY POINTS TO REMEMBER

- Your loved one may not recognize that she is struggling. She may believe that what she is experiencing is a normal part of motherhood or that she simply isn't any good at motherhood.
- By knowing what to look out for, you can help her to begin to recognize that there might be something more going on.

- Signs to look out for include: sleep disturbance (beyond what is normal with a baby); fatigue; lack of motivation; poor self-care with regards to personal hygiene and basic needs; struggling with a daily routine; avoiding people or being more withdrawn.
- Look out for your loved one 'putting on a brave face' – she may not want anyone to know that she isn't coping.
- Your loved one might experience mood fluctuations from crying more than usual to being easily irritated; more anxious than usual; or she may appear emotionally distant and detached.
- Your loved one's relationship with her baby is likely to be affected – either by being overly preoccupied with her baby, or being detached and avoidant.
- Your loved one's relationship with others may be affected. She may avoid seeing others, or she might be struggling to be by herself and constantly seeking reassurance from those around her.
- Your loved one will likely experience a number of negative thoughts about herself and her ability to mother her child. She will believe these thoughts, even when there is no evidence for them. She may even begin to question whether she should have had a baby, wish that she hadn't or believe that everyone is better off without her – in these cases, it is important to seek help immediately.

- It is tricky to separate out the different symptoms of PND/PPD – they interweave and impact on each other, so look at the overall picture. Remember that you know your loved one well and will be a good judge of whether her symptoms are 'normal motherhood' or something more.

As you can see, PND/PPD is a complex and distressing mental health difficulty. There is no one answer for how your loved one might be feeling or why, and it is not always straightforward to recognize. However, hopefully you are beginning to form a picture of what to look out for if you believe your loved one might be struggling with PND/PPD.

Next, we will look at some of the other factors that can contribute to PND/PPD – either in triggering this, or exacerbating the problem. In knowing some of the other contributing factors, you can be more equipped with what to look out for and how to begin helping your loved one. You will find more information on how to help and support your loved one in Chapters 6, 7 and 8 and if you feel you need to access some additional support now, you can find details of where to start in Chapter 10.

CHAPTER 3

WHAT ELSE MAY CONTRIBUTE?

Postnatal/postpartum depression is a problem that is intertwined and enmeshed in so many other areas of a new mother's life. Your loved one's symptoms can have a cyclical and knock-on effect to each other, which in turn can serve to maintain and worsen the problem. In this chapter, we look at some of the other factors that can maintain and worsen PND/PPD.

SLEEP DEPRIVATION

No one enjoys sleep deprivation (there's good reason why it has been proven to be used as an actual torture strategy) and it is undeniable that this part of parenthood sucks. Sleep deprivation can lead to fatigue, irritability, mood changes, memory and focusing issues, along with physical side-effects such as lower immunity, increased fat stores, weight gain, increased stress hormones, and an effect on our ability to learn and process information. Sleep deprivation can also make us less able to react quickly, make decisions and remain observant and alert. It has also been shown to increase the risk of depression, anxiety and, in extreme cases, psychosis. Chronic sleep deprivation has even been shown to shorten life expectancy.

So why are we talking about the awful impact of sleep deprivation? Well, sleep deprivation comes hand in hand with having a baby. Frequent night feeds, nappy changes, and rocking the baby to sleep cause significant disturbances to a new parent's sleep pattern. As well as this, Mother Nature seems to have played an especially cruel trick on mothers, who after the physical enormity of carrying and birthing a baby, are in the most need of rest than ever before. This is a potent combination for both the development of PND/PPD and the maintenance of it.

A woman who is vulnerable to PND/PPD needs more rest and yet it is the very thing she is unable to get. The chronic sleep deprivation when you have a newborn can be a triggering factor in the development of PND/PPD, but the ongoing nature of it, combined with sleeping too much or not being able to sleep, means that the cycle is maintained, and the symptoms worsen.

"Sleep was a huge factor for me in staying mentally healthy – so if my baby won't let me sleep, how can I ever feel mentally well?"
Polly

"The sleep deprivation was like torture and it made everything worse. I'd be so exhausted and then get angry with my baby, which then just made me feel so guilty."
Jen

FEEDING DIFFICULTIES

There are some differences in how a mum experiences feeding difficulties depending on whether she is bottle- or breastfeeding, but there are also many similarities. This section is not about which method of feeding is 'best', but an attempt to understand some of the difficulties faced by a new mother, depending on which way she has decided to feed her baby.

BREASTFEEDING MUMS

Breastfeeding is seen to be the 'natural way', but for many women it does not come naturally and is, in fact, very difficult. Breastfeeding difficulties not only leave a new mother vulnerable to feeling anxious about how much milk her baby is getting, but can also make her feel like a failure. Something that is seen to be so 'natural' shouldn't be so hard, right? Wrong!

"The self-blame from struggling with breastfeeding can make a new mother vulnerable to PND/PPD."

And yet, a new mother struggling to breastfeed will be quick to make this assumption. She will readily assume that she is the problem, that it is her fault for finding it hard, and that it is her who is failing at it. The reality is, breastfeeding is new to both mother and baby. While natural, it takes practice and learning. And that's not to mention other obstacles, including issues with milk production (due to a traumatic birth, being separated from the baby, poor health, etc.), tongue ties (which prevent the baby from feeding correctly), mastitis (a serious infection in the milk ducts), and a mother's or infant's ill health. The self-blame from struggling with breastfeeding can make a new mother vulnerable to PND/PPD due to self-criticism and feelings of failure, which along with everything else that a newborn brings, can be a perfect storm for PND/PPD.

"I remember thinking that breastfeeding was the most natural thing in the world and I couldn't even get that right – I felt like such a failure and like I'd let my baby down."
Jen

As if feeling like a failure isn't enough, let's consider what struggling with breastfeeding actually looks like in action. The mother feels anxious and stressed, the baby gets frustrated and hungry, the mum gets more anxious and stressed, the baby screams bloody murder because he or she is hungry – the mum then has a very normal reaction to that level of distress from her baby.

We are physiologically programmed to respond to our babies crying. The crying sends a signal to our brain that all is not OK, and due to this threat response our body then primes us to defend, protect and soothe our baby. When a hungry baby is screaming the house down, and a mum is struggling to breastfeed, a physiological alarm system goes off in her body which makes her very anxious and stressed. When she can't soothe her baby – in this case because of the struggle to breastfeed, it can feel catastrophic. Now an objective perspective on this allows us to see that this one particular feed is not life or death; that right now neither mother nor baby are in any real, immediate danger, but that is not what a mum's body or brain is telling her. As such, this can further exacerbate her negative mood and feelings of failure. If this is a persistent issue, the mother can become increasingly stressed and anxious about feeding and may see each 'failed' feed as evidence of her own failure.

To make matters worse, a screaming baby tends to attract attention from others – strangers staring or commenting, and well-meaning people offering feeding advice. The new mother may become anxious about feeding at all, or use it as another reason to withdraw from others, choosing to be alone to feed her baby. While this isn't problematic in itself, if she is struggling *and* withdrawing, it leaves her vulnerable to having a low mood and feeling isolated.

> "I remember a lady tutting at me in a café when I couldn't get my baby to latch on. I felt so self-conscious and got so anxious that it was all a big mess. I ended up balling my eyes out while still trying to feed my baby – I really struggled feeding in public again, and avoided going out at all if I could."
>
> Dara

'Grieving'

For women who are unable to continue breastfeeding, there is an extra layer of challenge. The body's response to no longer breastfeeding is to cease milk production. In the 'olden days' this physiological change in the early days of motherhood was probably due to the baby not surviving, and so the woman's body went through a grieving process. Motherhood has large primal and physical components, and so while nowadays the cessation of milk production is more likely related to a decision to switch to bottle-feeding, the woman's body may respond to this as having 'lost the baby', which can be very confusing and disorientating, and not always within a woman's consciousness.

"When we gave up breastfeeding, that's when things really went downhill. I felt like a failure, but I also felt like I was grieving it."
Chloe

HOW TO HELP

It is very important that your loved one feels able to openly talk about the challenges she is having with breastfeeding, and for this to be met with compassion and understanding. It is important that she is surrounded with reassurance that finding her feeding journey hard does not make her a failure – even if she hasn't said this out loud. Additionally, it is important that she is given space and support, but ultimately autonomy to decide whether breastfeeding is something she wishes to continue.

BOTTLE-FEEDING MUMS

With bottle-feeding, the physiological response to a hungry baby is the same as breastfeeding; the panic about the baby not taking enough milk is the same; the unwanted attention can be the same; the feelings of getting it wrong can be the same. Of course, there are differences between breast- and bottle-feeding, but that is not to say that difficulties with one are worse than difficulties with the other.

A bottle-feeding mum may feel guilty for not breastfeeding and feel she is being judged for this decision. She may be preoccupied with how much and how often her baby is feeding – sometimes having measurements can be more anxiety-provoking. There may be anxieties about the right kind of milk, bottles, teats, the right way to sterilize. All these anxieties can make a mother vulnerable to feeling like she is getting things wrong and questioning herself.

> "A bottle-feeding mum may feel guilty for not breastfeeding and feel she is being judged for this decision."

And on top of this, a bottle-feeding mum may find that she is just as indispensable as a breastfeeding mum if her baby will not take a bottle from anyone else, and so this can cause difficulties in sharing the load of feeding. Conversely, some babies might be more settled being bottle-fed by someone else (particularly in the early days) because the smell of mum leads to them refusing the bottle. This can be very distressing for the mum and can feel like rejection, which is difficult for any new mother, but dangerous for one who is already feeling inadequate.

"I felt like I couldn't escape. Even though my baby was bottle-feeding, my baby wouldn't take a bottle from my partner so I never got a break."
Kay

EXPRESSING MILK

Mothers who are expressing milk may feel detached from their babies. Expressing takes up a huge amount of time and energy and can result in someone else feeding the baby. As such, the mum may be missing out on those opportunities to hold her baby close, and if there are other risk factors for PND/PPD, this disconnection can be very damaging.

On top of this, expressing is probably the most time-consuming method of feeding with the time it takes to express, plus the need to store the milk correctly, wash and sterilize the breast pump, feed the baby, wash and sterilize the bottles – this method of feeding can feel utterly relentless, with no space in between. And this is all the more true if the baby demands to only be fed by the mum. It can exacerbate sleep deprivation and along with the feelings of disconnection, can be problematic for a mum's wellbeing.

"When I was expressing, I would sit there looking at my baby and just feel totally detached. I felt like a milking cow rather than a mum. My husband basically did all the caring while I sat and expressed. I felt totally useless, and it just created more distance between me and my baby."
Lucy

MUM GUILT

When a woman becomes a mother, it is as though she is presented with a baby, along with a lifetime's subscription of mum guilt that she didn't sign up for. There can be guilt about everything! This likely comes from a primitive need to keep the baby safe and well and to avoid danger – if we are hyper-critical of ourselves and our actions, we are less likely to make a mistake. This seems to make sense, except that this guilt can rob a mother of the reality of her life. It can tell her that she is getting something wrong, with no evidence for this at all. It can make a mother doubt and question herself – over everything! Mum guilt itself is not likely to cause PND/PPD, but the guilt a mother experiences for seemingly small things can add to the burden; it can give her the evidence she is looking for to confirm that she is indeed a failure. But we have to be careful with guilt – when we experience guilt we assume that we must have done something wrong, but there is a difference between feeling guilty and actually being guilty!

"Feelings of guilt can give her the evidence she is looking for to confirm that she is indeed a failure."

So, when your loved one is describing feeling guilty for something, think about whether she actually has anything to be guilty about and gently help her to see that probably it is just a feeling at play! It's also worth bearing in mind that she no doubt has too high expectations of herself, which may be contributing to the feelings of guilt – it's not that she's doing anything wrong, but simply that she is not meeting those 'too high' expectations.

"I felt guilty for EVERYTHING. Anything that went wrong, every time my baby cried, when my husband and I fought, when my eldest was sad – I just felt the guilt of everything! I even felt guilty for not being able to make the scrambled eggs properly!"

Maya

EXTERNAL PRESSURE

Everyone has an opinion about the right and wrong way to parent – offering advice on feeding, sleeping, soothing, cuddling, etc. In the early days of motherhood, women are especially vulnerable to external pressures on how things 'should be done'. And for women who may already be showing signs of PND/PPD, not living up to the expectations of those around her can be very damaging. Whether it be the 'well-meaning' grandparents and aunties, or the portrayals of perfect mums on Instagram, those external pressures have the potential to leave a new mother feeling not good enough.

HOW TO HELP

It can be helpful to mitigate these external influences by supporting your loved one in her decision-making. When she is feeling vulnerable and potentially very low and unsure of herself, she may not be able to speak up for herself. If, for example, grandma thinks that the baby is getting cuddled too much or someone comments that mum should be breastfeeding not bottle-feeding, speak up for her.

ISOLATION

At the time of writing this book, the world has been shaken by the Covid-19 pandemic resulting in lockdowns, restrictions and quarantines. These factors will certainly have taken their toll on many new mothers, but the resulting isolation is something that is a known factor in the development of PND/PPD *without* a global pandemic. Adapting to motherhood often means spending long spells of time alone with the baby – whether it is during those long nights with an unsettled baby, or those long days when a partner is at work.

> *"It was an incredibly isolating feeling – I just felt so on my own and like nobody cared."*
> Isla

While lots of mums manage to get out and about to baby classes and lunch dates with friends, this is not always possible, and is rarely easy. Having a fussy baby, difficulties breastfeeding, extreme sleep deprivation, and having few people to call on since most friends and family work, makes going out seem like a big chore, and so staying at home often seems like the easier option. But that isolation can leave a mother alone with those negative thoughts, and very little opportunity to challenge them or be distracted from them. In addition, isolation makes it even harder to open up about how she might be feeling, simply due to a severe lack of opportunity. The isolation also robs a mum of a supportive network of people who could make the motherhood more enjoyable.

"Isolation makes it even harder to open up about how she might be feeling, simply due to a severe lack of opportunity."

HOW TO HELP

To help support your loved one with isolation, you could:
- Check in with your loved one regularly with phone calls and messages
- Pop in on her if you can
- Help your loved one plan her day the night before so that she is getting out regularly
- Spend a little time in the morning supporting your loved one to get things organized for the day ahead

KEY POINTS TO REMEMBER

- A number of factors can impact on your loved one's experience of PND/PPD, which can maintain or worsen the problem. Knowing what to look out for, you can support your loved one with these additional factors to reduce their impact on her wellbeing.

- Sleep deprivation is a big factor in the development and maintenance of PND/PPD. While in part unavoidable with a baby, supporting your loved one to get as much rest as possible will be important for reducing its impact on her mental health.

- Feeding difficulties – struggling with breast, bottle, expressing, or a combination can feed into a mother's belief in herself. Being attuned to a mother's needs and wishes with regards to feeding and supporting her to make decisions based on these is important.

- Mum guilt is like signing up for a lifetime subscription no one asked for. This guilt can lead to your loved one being hyper-critical of herself and giving herself a hard time for things she has no reason to feel guilty for. While mum guilt is a normal part of most mothers' experiences, the guilt experienced by women suffering from PND/PPD is heightened and is used as evidence for how rubbish they are. Listen out for unreasonable guilt and challenge it when you hear it.

- Look out for any additional and unwanted sources of external pressure that might be impacting on your loved one. Whether it be the well-meaning auntie giving advice or the 'perfect mums' on social media, look out for these and reduce your loved one's exposure where you can, and speak up for her when she perhaps can't.
- Isolation can leave a mum struggling with PND/PPD especially vulnerable. She will lack support, and also be left alone with her own thoughts. Supporting her to be less isolated will be helpful in preventing this.

As you can see, PND/PPD is caused by, exacerbated by and maintained by a variety of complex, and often hidden, factors. In your supportive role, you are the first line of defence. Equipped with the information already presented, along with some practical tools and strategies coming up, you are well positioned to help your loved one avoid or recover from PND/ PPD. So, let's move on to have a look at your helping role.

CHAPTER 4

YOUR ROLE IN RECOVERY

It may be too much to expect your loved one to be able to separate herself from her experience and identify that something is wrong. Left to her own devices, it is likely that she will hit crisis point before it becomes apparent to her. That is why it is vital that you, as the person supporting her, have the insight to be able to identify when she might be struggling and to intervene early. It is likely that she will find it hard to articulate what she is feeling, and so in this chapter we are going to think about what she really needs you to understand, what she might need from you, and how you might begin to support her in her recovery.

And it doesn't just fall to one person to do this. If you are the partner, think about the other people that you might call upon to offer additional support. As the sayings go, 'No man is an island' and 'It takes a village to raise a baby'.

If you are her mother, sister or friend, for example, know that you can help and support your loved one too. It might be that she doesn't have a partner, or that her partner is unable to provide the support needed, for whatever reason.

"I knew I needed to have lots of patience and understanding and put her needs first. It wasn't easy, but seeing her so sad kept me motivated to make it better."
Caleb

THE ROLE OF THE PARTNER

As the partner, you are likely going to be the most important person in your loved one's recovery. You will be there during the night feeds, there when everyone else leaves, there when she can no longer pretend. You are the person who is going to be the most likely to notice the changes in her mood and behaviour and so you are the first line of defence. And you are the voice that can advocate on her behalf when she can't. You are also the person who can respond immediately, who can intervene when things get tough, and can lighten the load. You are the person who can love her unconditionally during a time when she potentially feels worthless. Your unwavering love and unconditional positive regard can be the reminder to her that the darkness she is in is not the reality. She will likely be all-consumed by that darkness, and she needs you to show her the way out. Now you might not have all the tools and equipment to pull her out of the darkness, but hopefully, with insight, understanding and a few tricks up your sleeve, you can help guide her to where she can get that help.

"You are the person who can love her unconditionally during a time when she potentially feels worthless."

"I saw my role as being a constant reminder to her that there was still a blue sky despite all the clouds she was seeing."
Dave

THE ROLE OF FRIENDS AND FAMILY

While it may not be quite as easy for you to support your loved one, given you aren't with her all the time, it is important to recognize that you still have a crucial role to play. You might be the safe space where she can open up about her experiences, if speaking to her partner feels too difficult. If you are a mother yourself, your experience of motherhood may be just what she needs to hear about to help her feel confident enough to express herself. Your role is going to be mainly focused around maintaining the contact and providing as much opportunity to notice her experience and struggles. It can be hard for you, as often it can feel like being left in the dark, but maintaining that contact and communication will be the main mechanism for you to offer support. Be prepared for it being you that needs to make the effort and keep putting the work in to maintain that contact.

"My sister tried to hide most of it from me. I was confused because I felt like I couldn't really relate, having never been through it, and she wasn't talking to me. It left me feeling really helpless and I couldn't really understand it. But I knew she needed me, so I just kept showing up and making her tea until she eventually broke down and told me what was going on."

Leah

BE A 'MIND READER'

For the most part, your loved one is going to need you to understand, even when she can't tell you how she is feeling. In many ways, she needs you to be the mind reader for her when she doesn't have the words. That is a lot to expect of you, but hopefully the information we've already covered, along with what's still to come, will help you feel more confident in this.

"I wish others knew how hard it is to admit to. Everything felt so much harder with PND/PPD – but asking for help felt almost impossible."
Catherine

A mother struggling with her mental health might feel unable to voice her thoughts and feelings, because in doing so she might believe she is admitting to being a bad mum. It can be a scary and lonely place, feeling that you have to put a brave face on, while being terrified that it might slip, while also being left alone to the sadness and distress within.

"It was an incredibly isolating feeling and a time filled with such hidden sadness."
Anna

"Just because someone looks 'fine', it's probably a front, because you're terrified of everything collapsing around you."
Megan

"I wish my husband could have 'read' when I needed that space or when I needed that hug."
Nadyia

BE PROACTIVE

Your loved one needs you to see beyond the mask she might be putting on. She needs you to be looking out for the signs that she isn't quite herself, but also to be proactive. In this kind of scenario, it's best to assume that she simply cannot start the conversation – either it is too hard or she hasn't quite recognized that something is wrong. You starting the conversation might just be the catalyst needed for her to open up and for the ball to start rolling in getting the help she needs.

"Overall, I think if just one of the people who 'had a hunch' had taken the time to actually check in more directly about PND/PPD, I wonder if I would have got help sooner."
Monica

"I wish someone had given me a chance to speak and to understand what I was feeling and why."
Catherine

"Your loved one needs you to see beyond the mask she might be putting on."

HOW TO HELP

It can be really hard to know what to say. You might be fearful of saying the wrong thing or upsetting your loved one more. Those worries are valid, but also should not stop you from starting this important conversation. Here are some opening phrases that might be useful:

- 'I've noticed that you've not quite been yourself and I'm worried that you're maybe not OK and not feeling able to tell me.'

- 'I know you might not feel able to speak to me about how you're feeling, but I want you to know, that no matter what you are thinking or feeling, I love you. I know that you are an amazing mother and nothing you tell me will change that.'

- 'I can tell that you are struggling and I want to be able to help you. It's OK if you are not feeling OK.'

- 'I know you've been struggling and giving yourself a hard time for that, but none of that makes you a bad mum. Maybe there is something else going on here, and maybe there are ways that I or others might be able to help you feel better.'

We will go into more detail about how to start this conversation and manage any resistance to it in Chapter 5.

GIVE PERMISSION

"I suspected that I had PND/PPD, but struggled to admit to myself that I was depressed. I'd tell health visitors and even my doctor numerous times that I was struggling and anxious, but could never say that I was depressed. They'd always say I looked great and was doing fine. My son was ten months old when I finally went to the doctor and told him I thought I had PND/PPD and wanted help."
Suri

Being told 'You are doing so well' and 'You look fine' might sound encouraging and reassuring to any mum, but one struggling with her mental health might view it as a barrier to opening up about how she is feeling. It is important to acknowledge to your loved one that it is OK for her not to be feeling fine.

While you might say, 'You are doing an incredible job,' you might follow it up with, 'But it's OK if you are finding this really hard.' It is not necessarily about taking away the encouragement or reassurance that she is doing better than she thinks, but about balancing this with permission to open up about how she is feeling.

Your loved one might be finding it difficult to even admit to herself that she is finding it hard, let alone voicing that to someone else. And so, in you voicing it for her and validating it as OK, you give her the opportunity and permission to say what's on her mind. You might also help her see that she doesn't need to suffer what she is experiencing, and that help might be available.

BE GENTLY PUSHY

"I wish people had been able to see past appearances – just because I looked fine and said I was fine, really didn't mean I was fine."
Nina

There is a good chance that even when you broach the subject, you might be met with, 'I'm fine.' It is entirely possible that your loved one is 'fine', but there is also a chance that this response is a way of avoiding the conversation. Remember, a mother struggling with her mental health is likely to be very committed to the idea that she is the problem, and that any admission of what she is feeling is going to result in others thinking she is a bad mother. So, she might need you to be a little pushy for her to trust that it is OK to open up.

> "Expect to be dismissed, but don't take that as proof that she's fine."

I say pushy, but what I really mean is 'gently pushy'. It is about acknowledging that this is really hard for her, but also staying committed to the conversation. Of course, we want to respect her and her choices about whether she wants to talk there and then, but if you get shot down in flames the first time, give her some space and come back to it later. Expect to be dismissed, but don't take that as proof that she's fine. Trust your instincts and what you know about your loved one; remind yourself of why you were concerned in the first place and keep in mind that she might just not be ready to tell you. If you back off after the first attempt, you may hijack any further opportunities for your loved one to open up when she feels a bit more ready. And the more opportunities you can give her, the more likely she is to trust that it is OK to open up.

It could be helpful to share why you are concerned with her and why you keep coming back to the topic; and keep telling her that no matter what she's going through, you are there to support her.

PICK UP THE SLACK

If your loved one is struggling with her mental health, and is experiencing thoughts of failure and inadequacy, she may try to compensate for this by trying to do everything. This is simply not achievable, especially when she is already sleep deprived, recovering from childbirth and adapting to life as a mother. You can be supportive by anticipating this and picking up the slack where you can. The anticipatory part of this can be quite important – assume that she probably won't ask you for your help, even if you offer it; assume that she has donned the superhero cape and is trying to prove she's good enough by running herself into the ground. Take the initiative – if you see the laundry is overflowing, put a load on; if you see dishes on the side, do them; if you know bedtime is a struggle, start the process; if you know she hasn't eaten today, make her something. Pick up the chores so that she doesn't have to and help her prevent herself from running herself into the ground.

> "You are challenging the idea that she 'must do it all', by removing some of those tasks."

By taking the initiative, you are removing a layer of expectation and guilt from her. You are challenging the idea that she 'must do it all', by removing some of those tasks, but you are also making it easier to accept as you are not asking her, nor is she needing to ask you. This subtle shift in picking up the slack can give her the much-needed space and time to focus on her own needs, while taking any guilt out of accepting the help because she didn't get a choice in the first place.

DON'T TAKE IT PERSONALLY

This part is *hard*! If your loved one is struggling with PND/PPD, the chances are she's taking this out on you in some way. Whether that's her being increasingly irritable with you, or withdrawn, or it feeling as though you can't do anything right because she gets upset or angry no matter what you do. It's natural that you might react to this and take it personally. But a lot of this behaviour won't be personal. It won't really be that you keep getting everything wrong, but more that her internal experiencing is spilling out over the top. Try to remember that it is PND/PPD rather than your loved one making her behave in the way she is.

Unfortunately (for you) this is a really normal occurrence. We often take out our emotional experiencing on those closest to us. The reason for this is because you are probably the safest person she can do that with. You are the person she trusts the most and who she trusts will not abandon her. I know that doesn't make it easier for you in those moments, but knowing that this is an expression of her distress might help you create a little bit of distance between her behaviour and your natural, instinctive response – remember that it is PND/PPD, not your loved one.

If you respond to her behaviour defensively, then it's probably not going to make the situation better. Now that's not to say you must sit there and be her punching bag, that's not helpful either. But it is about seeing those punches as wild, uncontained and uncontrollable, rather than seeing them as being directed at you specifically. Knowing how to look after yourself when this happens is important, and something we will cover in Chapter 9.

"It's hard to control that deep sense of wanting to be alone and tolerating people. I wished my partner knew that it wasn't personal."
Nadyia

"It was like living with someone who you care about, but who used you like a punching bag, and needing to be OK with that."
Dave

"It wasn't always easy not to react when she started having a go at me. To begin with, I did get angry about it, but I realized that just made everything worse."
Lee

HOW TO HELP

Rather than getting angry at your loved one's outbursts, take a step back, take a breath, and remind yourself that this is not the usual way she behaves, nor is it a reflection on you. You might take a moment to reflect on what the outburst was about – consider ways you could help more, perhaps by taking over some of the night feeds, for example. Respond to that, but don't go down the rabbit hole of you now not being enough.

BE RELENTLESSLY ON HER SIDE

Your loved one might be feeling as though it's her against the world. She might believe that everyone is ready to judge and criticize her and might feel that she has no one on her side. Your role is to be relentlessly on her side. Even when she doesn't necessarily need you to be; even when you might not agree with something she does or says; letting her know that you are always on her side and that you always have her back is so important.

"Having my husband's and his mum's unconditional support was the most helpful thing for me. They never questioned what I was feeling; they were just there for me when it was all too much."
Petra

There is a good chance that the way your loved one is seeing the world and people is distorted. Her trust in others to understand and not judge might be lacking, and so she may assume that no one would understand if she were to voice her feelings. Similarly, she is likely to assume that other people will be thinking the same way that she is about her mothering – if she believes she is a failure as a mother, there is a high chance she believes that's what you think too.

> "Letting her know that you are always on her side and that you always have her back is so important."

We've spoken about the fact that she will likely find it difficult to talk about any of these things, and so your job is to challenge these assumptions before they get a chance to take hold and show her you are on her side. Being the person she can lean on will help her gain trust in you always having her back.

- Reassure her that you think she is a brilliant mother.
- Tell her that it is OK to be struggling.
- Step in when she is receiving unwanted 'advice'.
- Speak up for her, especially when other people aren't listening.

- Validate her experiences.
- Help her to seek support.
- Advocate for her when she can't.

BE HONEST

Perhaps slightly in opposition to the previous point about being on your loved one's side, one of the roles you might have is to talk honestly with others about what is going on at home. Imagine the following scenario ...

You attend the six-week postnatal check and your loved one tells the doctor, 'I'm fine, everything is good,' but you know she has been crying a lot and not looking after herself properly. You notice that her cheery disposition is a sharp contrast to how she was five minutes before she arrived. And you notice she hasn't said a word about that.

Your role is first to try to help your loved one open up about what's really been going on – perhaps by saying, 'Are you sure? You have been quite upset at times.' Hopefully this will be enough to encourage her to start talking, or for the doctor to pick up that all is not quite as it seems and to probe a little more.

If that doesn't happen, which is quite possible, you might need to be a little more direct: 'Well, actually, I'm a little concerned. She seems to be struggling and finding it hard to talk about it.' Now your loved one might not thank you for this initially and might think this is you not being on her side but, in fact, this is you advocating for the part of her that can't speak up. It is you being relentlessly on her side, not the side of her inner critic who doesn't want anyone to know the truth.

"I knew she was going to be really angry with me for telling the health visitor, but by that point I knew we needed more help. Even though she was pretty annoyed, when we all spoke about it, she was able to see why I was so concerned, and eventually forgave me."

Ryan

Sometimes your role might be in speaking the words that your loved one really doesn't want spoken. But remember, the longer it stays hidden and the longer your loved one goes without the support she needs, the harder it will get. Being able to speak honestly to health professionals and trusted family and friends is going to be a central role of yours, and possibly one of the hardest given that you are likely to be met with a lot of resistance. Trust that when she is out of the other side of the PND/PPD, she will be glad that you spoke up for her and pushed her to get the help she needed.

KNOW WHEN TO ASK FOR HELP

Knowing when you can no longer, alone, meet your loved one's needs, and knowing when to ask for help is important. She may never take that step, but that doesn't mean that you shouldn't. You may be met with resistance, but trust that you are seeking the help because she can't; not necessarily because she doesn't want or need it.

> "Knowing when you can no longer, alone, meet your loved one's needs, and knowing when to ask for help is important."

It Is easy to put off asking for help and wait for things to get better. You might find yourself saying things like, 'I'll give it until the weekend' or 'This is just a difficult week, it'll get better.' And while this might be true, after all caring for a baby is hard work, if you are seeing some of the signs and symptoms listed earlier (see Chapter 2), then it's best not to put off seeking help as it will give your loved one the best chance of a quicker recovery, and ultimately wrestle her motherhood experience back from the grips of PND/PPD. If in doubt, keep this in mind – earlier is always better.

"At our one-year check, my health visitor admitted to me that she had been worried about me in the early days. I remember thinking, 'Why didn't you say anything?' Maybe if she had, I might have been able to hear it."
Orla

OTHER IMPORTANT ROLES

As we've already said, no man is an island, and so it is important to recognize that other people might be able to step in and offer support. In some circumstances, going over your partner's head to seek support from others might not be the wisest of ideas, but trust that while she might initially be annoyed with you, in the long run, when she can see things a little more clearly, she will recognize that it is exactly what she needed.

Knowing who to call on is important too. Ensure that you are reaching out to the people you think your loved one would want to be there in a time of need. Think about how understanding and empathic those others are and consider wisely who you might reach out to. If you are the partner, you might, for example, confide in her mother or another close family member. It could be her own mother, sister, auntie, friend or mother-in-law. If you are her mother, you might, for example, let one of her closest friends know. Speaking to other mothers may help her feel less alone and a little more understood. However, be wary of comparisons – your loved one will readily compare herself against anyone she thinks is doing a better job than her. Be sure to talk openly and honestly about the challenges of motherhood for yourself too, to help normalize her experience.

Seeking this help is vital for you too, so that you don't burn yourself out trying to do it all, because there will be times when you alone simply cannot meet all your loved one's needs. As a partner, for example, you might reach out to her mother to help out with the baby and household chores. You might ask someone to come and stay for a few nights to help out with those sleepless nights, or you might ask them to take the baby for a walk so that you can both get some rest.

It is also important to remember the impact on you as the helper. Whether that be worrying about your loved one, carrying the extra load from picking up the slack, or, if you're the partner, simply your own adjustment into parenthood, recognizing that you have needs that matter too is going to be crucial for you to be able to offer effective support. The saying 'You can't pour from an empty cup' is so very true, and so for you to be able to look after your loved one, you also need to look after yourself.

KEY POINTS TO REMEMBER

- Additional support from those around her is going to be crucial for your loved one's wellbeing and recovery from PND/PPD.

- This doesn't fall to any one person; her partner, mother, sister or friend all have a vital role in being able to help – so enlist more support where you can.

- As a partner, you are likely to be the first line of defence, while also being her advocate. You have the advantage of being around your loved one more than anyone else.

- As friends and family, while you may not be around quite so much, you can be a safe place for her to open up to. Maintaining contact and providing opportunities for her to talk is going to be central to your role in your loved one's recovery.

- Your loved one is going to need lots of understanding from you, even when she isn't able to express exactly what is going on. She is, in some ways, going to need you to be her 'mind reader'.

- Your loved one needs you to be proactive in addressing the PND/PPD.

- She needs you to make it OK that she doesn't feel OK. Validate her experience and give her the permission to feel however she is feeling.

- Your loved one needs you to be pushy. Don't be too quick to be brushed off by 'I'm fine'. Gently revisit the conversation and share your concerns with her.
- Your loved one needs you to take the initiative and pick up the slack – don't let the housework build up around her for her to feel more of a failure. Anticipate this and remove this layer of expectation and guilt from her.
- Your loved one needs you to understand that she is struggling with her mental health, and so to not take her behaviour or moods personally. Remember that it is the PND/PPD, not your loved one.
- Your loved one needs you to be relentlessly on her side – she needs to know you have her back and will support her, regardless of how she is feeling.
- Your loved one will need you to be honest with her. Tip-toeing around your concerns won't get her the support she needs.
- Your loved one won't always know when she needs extra help, or be able to ask for it. She needs you to know when to call in more support.
- Calling in the cavalry, and getting extra support, will not only be beneficial for your loved one, but will also help you in your supporting role.

Now that you have a better sense of your role in your loved one's recovery, let's move on to consider how you begin to communicate with your loved one what your concerns are and how to move forward toward helping her.

CHAPTER 5

STARTING THE CONVERSATION

Talking to your loved one about her mental health may feel daunting. Understandably you might be concerned about upsetting her, that she might hear your concerns as criticism, that you might be met with resistance or that she will withdraw further. While these are all valid concerns, they are not reasons to put off having the conversation. Talking is going to be an important step toward your loved one being able to open up about how she is feeling, and then accessing the right support, and ultimately recovering.

It is key to plan the conversation as best as you can to balance the need to communicate your concerns, While protecting your loved one from feeling judged or criticized. Bear in mind that acknowledging that there is a problem, believing it and seeing it in herself might be really confronting and upsetting for her, so being able to do this sensitively is crucial. No small task, eh?! In this chapter, we explore ways to approach the conversation, what to avoid and how to manage resistance.

MANAGE YOUR OWN EMOTIONS

First, check in with your own emotions. As you enter a potentially difficult conversation, you need to feel calm and be clear about what you want to say. It's natural for you to be having your own emotional experiences in relation to your loved one's difficulties, and while this is completely valid, it is important that those heightened emotions can be contained as much as possible.

Your loved one might get angry, upset or defensive – if she does, it is important to stay calm and grounded and not take it personally. It might be that you have someone there to support you, but ensure that your loved one feels cared for rather than ganged up on. We cover how you can look after yourself in Chapter 9, so you might want to have a look over those strategies before approaching the conversation.

PLAN WHAT YOU WANT TO SAY

Being clear about what you want to communicate and why will help you to stay calm and continue the conversation, even if it gets difficult. Write a few pointers down for yourself around the main messages you want to get across, and what you would like to achieve:

Some of the areas you might want to cover include:

- Your concerns about your loved one's wellbeing.
- That you've noticed a change in her mood.
- That you have noticed that she seems to be struggling.
- That you think she might benefit from having someone to talk to.
- That you love her and are there for her.
- That you know, despite how she's feeling, that she's doing a great job, but might need some more help.
- To normalize PND/PPD and to communicate that it's OK to be struggling.

You might also want to write down what you want the next steps to be after the conversation, e.g. going to the doctor together to chat it through; calling the health visitor; finding a support group; letting close family know.

"As you enter a potentially difficult conversation, you need to feel calm and be clear about what you want to say."

You might also include some important steps toward helping your loved one now – e.g. ensuring she gets sufficient rest and how you might begin to achieve that; encouraging her to get out a little more; seeking the support of friends; trying to establish more of a routine, etc. You can find more on this in Chapter 6.

COMMUNICATE SENSITIVELY

Remember that your loved one is likely to be feeling pretty rubbish about herself, so it's important to strike a balance between communicating your concerns while remaining empathic and understanding. Being clear about your concerns while avoiding judgement is important. You want your loved one to know, above all else, that you are having this conversation because you are concerned about her wellbeing, not because you think she is a bad mum, or that she is doing something wrong. You might even pre-empt this by explicitly telling her that you think she's doing great, or that you don't want her to think that you are judging her. Often being explicit about some of those assumptions she might be making can help to challenge them, while also giving you room to get your concerns across – e.g. 'I know you might hear this as me saying you're a bad mum, but I do not believe that for a second. I am just worried about your wellbeing.'

It can also be helpful to communicate that this is your experience of the situation and that you are wanting to understand hers. Again, this avoids judgement, and allows space for her to expand on your concerns. Using phrases such as, 'I get the sense that ...' or 'I am concerned about you because ...' rather than 'You are depressed' or 'You aren't coping,' can help to position these concerns as yours, rather than an attack, and your loved one is likely to be more receptive to this.

Some physical contact might be helpful, too – holding her hand or sitting close by her. The proximity you create can help your loved one feel safe and contained and promote effective communication – you are literally by her side through this. It also means you are readily on hand to give her a hug if she needs it!

LISTEN – REALLY LISTEN

While you want your loved one to hear your concerns, this is also an opportunity for you to hear what's going on for her. She may not be able to tell you exactly how she is feeling, but it is important to listen closely to what she says. If she feels that you are not listening properly, then she is unlikely to continue talking. Bear in mind these active listening skills:

- **Maintain good eye contact:** This doesn't mean staring her out, but rather being free of distractions as much as possible, sitting so you can look at her, remaining attentive, even if she doesn't look at you.

- **Body language:** Reading your loved one's body language can be tricky, but noticing that she looks agitated or withdrawn, even if she is saying she is fine, gives you an opportunity to reflect that you can tell something is not quite right. Being aware of your own body language is also important. Ensuring that you have an open posture, are turned toward her and possibly leaning forward can show her that you are fully focused on her.

- **Encouragement:** Encourage her by smiling, nodding your head, and mirroring her where appropriate. You might use gentle encouragers like 'Mmm' or 'Oh right …' to help her begin to elaborate further, or simply ask her to tell you a little more.

- **Don't interrupt:** If your loved one is talking, it's important you don't talk over her, as she will not feel like you are really listening. Giving her the time and space to express how she is feeling, even if you don't agree with what she is saying, is important. Wait until there is a natural pause to say something.

- **Reflect it back:** Active listening often involves reflecting what you've heard and can be helpful in four ways:
  1) It helps you to clarify that you have understood what your loved one has said.

2) It shows that you have heard her.
3) It gives her the opportunity to hear her words back, which can be especially useful because it helps her hear those overly critical or irrational thoughts more objectively.
4) It gives her the opportunity to correct you or elaborate further – and anything that encourages her to open up more is good.

VALIDATE HER EXPERIENCE

Even though you probably won't agree with much of what your loved one thinks of herself, comments such as 'You're not a bad mum' or 'Don't be silly', while being well-meaning, can leave your loved one feeling unheard and invalidated. It's important to validate her experience, while gently challenging it. Validate that her experience is very real, and that her anxiety and distress are real, before challenging any of the unhelpful thoughts.

Statements such as, 'I can hear that you're really worried about not getting it right' or 'I know this feels really overwhelming for you' can help your loved one to know that you are hearing her experience. It doesn't mean that you then agree with her about what she is saying, but simply that you have heard and understood her. It can also be helpful for you to share some of your experience if appropriate. If your loved one describes feeling lost and not knowing what to do, it is likely you've felt the same way in those early days of parenthood. If you're her partner, being able to say, 'I'm terrified of getting it wrong too' or if you're her mother or a friend, 'I remember feeling that way as well when I had a baby' can help to normalize some of her experience and shows that you understand some of it.

"The most helpful thing was people who listened and helped me find ways of getting better."
Anna

> "Validate that her experience is very real, and that her anxiety and distress are real, before challenging any of the unhelpful thoughts."

AVOID CRITICISM

Avoid making any kind of judgement or being critical. Remember that your loved one is already feeling like a failure and so any addition to this is going to make her feel worse. Being sure to label your concerns as 'yours', rather being directed toward her can be really helpful. So rather than 'You're not coping,' use phrases such as 'I'm concerned that you might not be feeling like you're coping.' Or rather than 'You're not looking after the baby,' say something like 'I can see that you're feeling overwhelmed when you've got baby.' It might seem like a game of semantics, but the language you use is really important. Remember that your loved one will be hyper-vigilant to any signs that you think she isn't good enough, is a failure or a bad mother – because she is already thinking those things and her brain is biased to look for evidence to confirm those beliefs.

Highlight the concerns you have about her wellbeing, rather than it being specifically about what she is or is not doing. Balancing this with ongoing reassurance about your belief in her and your desire to support her will help with this. And if she does feel criticized, it will be important to acknowledge this, but reinforce that you are only concerned about her – e.g. 'I know you feel angry with me and think I'm criticizing you, and I'm sorry for that, but I really do think we need to look at getting some more support to help you feel better.'

"I was really worried about speaking to my wife about what I was seeing. I was worried I was going to make everything worse, that she was going to hate me, or that she might think I thought she wasn't a good mum. But after speaking to my own therapist about it, I realized that I couldn't put it off. I figured out what I wanted to say and how I wanted to say it. It ended up going well and my wife agreed to see a doctor."

Michael

WHAT YOU MIGHT HEAR

It is difficult to predict how your loved one will respond. She might be very receptive and grateful for the opportunity to talk openly; she might get angry and defensive and deny that there is anything wrong; or her response may be somewhere in the middle. Managing your own emotions in the moment is important, so that you are less likely to react to any heightened emotions in an unhelpful way.

If she is receptive, you might hear her sharing her internal thoughts, along with a sense of helplessness. She might say things like, 'I just don't know what's wrong with me,' or 'I don't know what to do.' This helplessness can be upsetting, but having gone in with a plan will mean you can support her through that helplessness by reassuring her that there are things that can be done to help.

Your loved one might try to get out of the conversation all together by attending to the baby, or suddenly needing the toilet. She might say she's too busy or tired to talk. You could gently challenge that avoidance by saying, 'I know this is really hard to talk about' or 'I know you maybe don't want to talk about this, but I think it's really important.' Allowing her to avoid the conversation is only going to prolong things, so being able to be empathic, while also gently pushing the conversation along, will be helpful.

If she is struggling to communicate, perhaps being very withdrawn (you might not even be sure she is listening) or very distressed (she might be very tearful), then it is important to attend to that emotional state first. If she is very distressed, then you might want to hold her, tell her it's OK, reassure her that you are there for her, and try to work on calming her down before proceeding with the conversation – but do proceed. If she is totally detached from you, then it will be important to establish the contact first – hold her hand, ask her to look at you, be close to her so that she feels safe. In this instance, you might need to share your concerns with her regardless of her input. It might be that she needs to hear your concerns and then have a bit of time before being able to respond to them. In this case, give her that space once you have shared your concerns, and then go back to her at a later point to follow up.

> "Creating an argument with you about something else avoids the real issue."

If your loved one becomes angry and defensive, keeping on top of your own emotional responses will really come into play. She may get angry and lash out at you. She might say things like, 'So you think I'm a terrible mum' or 'You don't support me; I'm doing this all myself.' The chances are this is just a defence mechanism kicking in – creating an argument with you about something else avoids the real issue. Staying calm and coming back to your concerns and your desire to support her will hopefully help her to feel less threatened. Seeing this anger as a reaction to her anxiety is helpful, as it will allow you to understand why she feels threatened – either that she will get found out, or that she feels criticized or judged.

Statements such as 'I know you're scared and angry, that's OK, but I love you and I'm concerned about you,' or 'I know you are finding this conversation hard, but I am not criticizing you for a second ... I just want to support you' can help to neutralize some of the anger. There is also a degree of preparing yourself to ride the wave of the anger. Your loved one's threat system might be very heightened, and the anger is a way of protecting herself. However, if you can stay calm, consistent, and there with her during that, she will realize that you are a safe place. However, patience and hanging on in there might be required.

FACING RESISTANCE

There is a chance that you'll be met with some resistance – either a denial of there being an issue, or an acceptance of the issue, but refusal to do anything about it. This can be difficult to manage, given that you are so concerned.

Denial is likely to stem from either fear of admitting there is a problem or being so caught up in the guilt and shame because she cannot see any other explanation than it being her fault. You can help by reassuring her that she has nothing to feel ashamed or guilty for. Be explicit that you do not think this is about her, but rather that she is suffering with PND/PPD, and perhaps sharing some of the understanding you have gained from this book. Often when shame and guilt get in the way, a woman will personalize her experience – 'I feel guilty, therefore I must be guilty.' However, if you can frame her symptoms and experiences within the context of the depression, it might give her an external explanation for her difficulties, rather than assuming it's her fault. Normalizing her experiences, but also emphasizing that help is available, will potentially make it feel safer for her to acknowledge that there is an issue.

"Remember that the resistance is likely a symptom of her difficulties rather than being how she really feels."

If your loved one does not wish to seek external support, or is unwilling to engage in any support at home, you may feel at a loss for what to do next. Being consistently supportive, implementing some of the strategies we will discuss in Chapter 7, and repeatedly coming back round to the idea of accessing more support will be helpful. Your loved one might not listen the first time, but if you persevere she might begin to realize that some help would be beneficial.

Overall, when it comes to managing resistance, it is important not be disheartened or put off and try to manage your frustration. Remember that the resistance is likely a symptom of her difficulties rather than being how she really feels. Giving her some space to reflect on what you've said, and then revisiting the discussion again fairly soon after, will make it difficult for her to continue to avoid the subject, and she is more likely to acknowledge her need for some more support. However, if you feel like you are really getting nowhere, then it might be that you take the initiative to access the support yourself. Talking to your family doctor, health visitor or a close family member might support you in getting her to engage in some support. We will cover how to get help more in Chapter 10.

MANAGING RISK

If during your conversation, your loved one begins to get very distressed and describes thoughts that make you worry about her immediate wellbeing – either threatening to harm herself or her baby, or doing something drastic, then it is important to know who to turn to. If she is expressing suicidal thoughts or you believe her to be a risk to herself or others, then you should call your family doctor or emergency services straight away. She might be really angry with you, but the safety of her and the baby is of the utmost importance. Remember that her reactions are related to her illness rather than how she truly feels, and they are hopefully temporary. When she is feeling in a better place and getting the support she requires, she will forgive you and likely be glad that you intervened when you did.

"I spoke to my wife on a few occasions about her mood, but she always said she was fine. I ended up speaking to her mum about it and she ended up talking to her. After that, she seemed to be able to open up a little more to me and we started figuring things out."
David

KEY POINTS TO REMEMBER

- Being able to talk to your loved one about your concerns and guide her toward getting some more support is a crucial step in her recovery; however, this can feel like a daunting process.
- It is important to balance sharing your concerns, while protecting your loved one from feeling judged or criticized.
- Before you have the conversation, check in with your own emotions; trying to have this challenging conversation and managing your loved one's emotions during this will be impossible if you are not on top of your own emotions.

- Plan what you want to say in advance; perhaps write down the main points you want to convey and what you want the next steps to be.
- Keep empathy and understanding high on the agenda. Your loved one will be highly sensitive to any perceived judgement – communicate sensitively.
- The conversation is an opportunity for you to hear your loved one's inner thoughts and feelings, so make sure to listen closely.
- Even though you may not agree with how she sees things, be sure to validate her experience – while it might not be true, it feels true for her and that must be really painful!
- Be mindful of any kind of criticism – consider carefully how you frame some of your concerns so that they are free of judgement and focused on your loved one's wellbeing.
- Your loved one may respond to this conversation in a variety of different ways – perhaps angry and defensive, or she may be very receptive and relieved to be able to talk openly. Or she may try to avoid the conversation all together, or get too distressed to engage. Being patient, managing your own emotions, and remembering that your loved one is struggling with PND/PPD will help you to step back from her reactions and figure out how to proceed.
- If there is lots of resistance, understanding that shame and guilt may be fuelling this is helpful.

- Implementing ongoing and consistent support (as outlined in the next chapters) will help you encourage her toward a place where she might resist further support less.
- Do not give up on her if there is lots of resistance. Remember that this is more likely a symptom of the PND/PPD than it is of her true feelings. Keep coming back to the conversation, or seek some additional support yourself.
- If there is any risk of harm indicated during this conversation, seek professional support immediately, even if your loved one gets angry.

Hopefully you have the beginnings of a plan for how to start the conversation with your loved one about her difficulties and potentially have even taken the plunge to start this conversation off. Next, we begin to explore some practical support that you can offer to help her in her recovery.

CHAPTER 6

PRACTICAL SUPPORT

We've spoken about your role in your loved one's recovery, but in this chapter we are going to expand on some of the specific practical ways that you might be able to help. Much of the advice here is basic, and likely things you are already doing and aware of. However, sometimes we underestimate the power of basic support, or even overlook this entirely!

If your loved one is struggling with postnatal/postpartum depression, dirty dishes or a full bin (things she has never been bothered about before) might be the thing to send her over the edge of her emotional capacity. By supporting her in practical ways, you can begin to take some of the load off of her, but you can also give her some more space to focus on her own needs.

"At the worst point of the PND/PPD, I remember coming downstairs to make a cup of tea – the baby was sleeping for a change – but there were no clean cups, the

dishwasher hadn't been put on, and I just burst into tears. Everything felt just too damn hard – even cleaning a cup. It feels surreal now – it was only a cup. But at the time, I just couldn't cope with it."

Lucy

Your loved one may not readily accept your practical support, perhaps because she thinks she needs to do it all herself; it will be important for you to challenge her refusal of this by taking the initiative and being assertive with her. However, you also want to help your loved one without disempowering her. If you charge in and take over everything, there is a risk she will feel unable to cope with anything. The aim is to make life easier for her, so that she might be able to look after herself a bit more without feeling so overwhelmed.

Another consideration when offering practical support is to ensure you are not facilitating a mother to disengage with her baby any further. If your loved one is avoiding her baby or allowing others to take over, then your practical support needs to be focused on how you help her to look after her baby, to build her confidence, but also to promote the bond between them.

So while offering practical support might seem obvious and basic, it's not quite so straightforward when we are supporting someone with PND/PPD. Whether you are the partner or a visitor, knowing what practical support could be prioritized can be really beneficial in supporting your loved one in her recovery.

HELPING THE MOTHER

The biggest thing your loved one needs right now is support. She needs you to sit with her while she is struggling to feed the baby, or while she cries. She needs you to be there for her, even when she doesn't ask. She needs you to visit, even when she seems to be avoiding your calls. Remember that she is likely to shut herself off from people and support, so showing up, whether she has asked you to or not, can be helpful. Call her on your lunch break, or swing by to check in on her. These little acts of connection will help her to remember that she is not alone. Another thing you can do is to make sure she is eating and drinking well. Bring her lunch and a glass of water or leave a sandwich in the fridge with a little reminder to eat.

Helping her get more sleep is one of the most helpful things you can do if she is struggling with her mental health. Offering to take baby for a few hours while she naps or taking over the night feeds to help out can be really beneficial. It might be that you offer to stay over and have baby in with you, or even just be there in those dark hours to support her while she is feeding and be on hand to help with the nappy changes and burping.

HOW TO HELP

- If she is sleeping too much, and you're noticing she is struggling to get out of bed, gently encouraging a routine might be helpful.
- Before you head off to work, or perhaps when you go round to visit, open the curtains, run the shower, take out some clothes and encourage her each step of the way.
- Prepare some breakfast and coffee downstairs, and again, encourage her each step of the way.
- Offer (or insist) to go out for a walk with her to get some fresh air.
- Invite a friend round who you trust to be understanding and who might distract her for a while.

Getting the balance between rest and routine is tricky, but remember that you know your loved one, and so trust your instincts about what she might be needing. If she is absolutely sleep deprived, then encourage more rest; however, if she is using her bed and sleep as a way of avoiding the world, then encourage more activity and routine.

HELP WITH BABY

Feeding, soothing, changing and caring for the baby are all different areas that you can help with, and in doing so you will not only give your loved one a much-needed break, you can also give her the space to begin looking after herself a little better.

However, this isn't necessarily simple. As previously mentioned, if your loved one is struggling to let anyone near her baby, or is disengaged from her baby, the support you offer in helping to look after baby needs to be carefully considered.

HELP WITH FEEDING

Feeding can be a difficult area for a mum struggling with PND/PPD, as discussed in Chapter 3, so if you are offering practical support here, be mindful of your loved one's own circumstances. If the mother is especially anxious about you helping with feeding, then stay in the same room initially as you offer the baby a bottle. Allow her to be close by if she feels she needs to intervene, but perhaps give her a blanket and pop on the TV. Hopefully, as she sees baby is OK, she will relax a little more and you'll be able to take baby into another room to give her some time to rest. If you are going to do a few feeds, then encourage her to go for a nap – perhaps on the sofa initially, but then encourage her to go to bed.

If she is more disengaged from baby, then your support would be more suited to encouraging her to feed baby herself – make it easy for her by making the bottles up or if she's breastfeeding, help her by bringing a drink and snack or help her get comfortable with pillows, blankets, etc.

BABYCARE

If your loved one is breastfeeding or she doesn't want (or need) help with feeding, then you could be on hand to help to wind baby and change any nappies. However, again, bear in mind that if mum is really anxious, it's best to stay close by; while if she is more disengaged, it may be about bringing the nappies and muslins to her and being with her as she changes baby.

As a partner, helping with the baby during the night is something that you can offer that visitors cannot, and is possibly one of the most helpful things you can do. While this might seem obvious, if mum doesn't outright ask for help, you might think she is coping OK during the night. Remember that some women with PND/PPD won't admit or show that they are struggling because they believe they need to be able to do it all themselves. So, if you think your loved one is struggling with PND/PPD, be careful not to make any assumptions about how she is fairing at night. Take the initiative (so she doesn't need to ask) and take over some of the feeds, or bring baby to mum and then sort baby out after.

By being proactive, you take some of the load off mum, without her having to ask. Even simply getting up when she is up feeding, so that you are on hand to help with nappy changes or projectile vomit, will offer practical support that you wouldn't be able to offer if you slept through the night feeds.

Another practical thing you can do to support her is to take the baby out for a walk for an hour so that your loved one can get some sleep or simply rest. Remember that your loved one might feel guilty for napping if she is struggling with PND/PPD so be sure to encourage her to make use of this break to catch up on rest. Put her to bed before you head out, or ensure that she is settled on the sofa and reassure her that having a nap is OK, because while we all know this to be true, her PND/PPD mindset will litter this simple act with doubt and guilt. If mum is too anxious for you to leave the house with baby, get her settled in her bed, while you cuddle baby in the living room or pop into the garden.

If the baby is unsettled, it can be particularly triggering for a mother struggling with PND/PPD. Helping her to stay calm while she tries to soothe her baby, either by reassuring her that she is doing a great job, or simply just being with her through the cries will feel supportive. But if she is really struggling, gently, and without judgement, step in. Just be careful not to make your loved one feel like she 'can't do it'. If mum is especially anxious, she might find this really difficult, as remember that a woman struggling with PND/PPD is highly sensitive to judgement or criticism. So be mindful that this could trigger your loved one's feelings of failure. Reassure her that she is doing a great job, but ask if she would like some help, or gently encourage her to take a break and let you take over. Perhaps take the baby to another room.

"The most helpful thing anyone did for me when I was really struggling with PND/PPD was allowing me to get some rest. My mum took the baby off me early in the morning to let me get a lie-in."
Abigail

However, if you do support her with the baby, and she has some time to herself, bear in mind that she might fill this time with other 'chores'; so perhaps run her a bath before you take over, or set her up with some food and her favourite TV show. By giving her a focus on how to spend that time on herself, she is more likely to engage in some self-care.

HELP MAKE THINGS EASY

A big challenge when someone is struggling with PND/PPD is the initiation of tasks – whether that be to get showered, or to make something to eat. Self-care becomes the lowest of priorities, so this is an area you can help to make a little easier. This will be especially true if your loved one is at home alone.

- You might take over the baby duties and run mum a bath or a shower before you head off to work or when you pop round to visit.

- You might batch-cook some meals that can be stored in the freezer so little thought or effort is required to make sure mum is eating something nutritious.
- You might ensure that there are sufficient groceries in the cupboards, organize for shopping to be delivered or indeed, take the responsibility to go and get the essentials.

Giving your loved one opportunities to look after herself gives her the best chance of engaging in self-care – this helps to make her feel more in control and ultimately more accomplished and empowered.

ACTIVITY DIARY

As I've highlighted previously, your loved one is potentially struggling to maintain a self-care routine and things like eating and sleeping may be affected. She may also be avoiding going out, being left alone with the baby – as well as avoiding other people. Being able to help her establish more of a routine and activity into her life can help her to feel that she has a little more control over her days.

"Being able to help her establish more of a routine can help her to feel that she has a little more control over her days."

A day at home with a baby by yourself may feel very overwhelming and daunting for your loved one. Helping her to plan her day can give her some sense of power rather than fear. You might help her write a few things down, or you can use the planner below to help structure her day. The aim is to get a balance of activity, rest, basic needs and enjoyable activities. People who are significantly struggling with PND/PPD can often benefit from more detail and smaller time frames (e.g. hour by hour, rather than morning, afternoon, evening).

Here's an example that accounts for all the basic needs of eating, rest, social contact, productivity and self-care. Of course, every person and baby is different, and babies so often love to throw a curveball (or dirty nappy) into the mix so stay flexible!

Time	Activity
8am	Get up, shower, get dressed while partner feeds baby before work
9am	Have breakfast, get baby dressed
10am	Walk with baby – nap time, meet a friend (already arranged)
11am	Feed baby, have snack and cup of tea
12pm	Baby nap time, lunch
1pm	Own nap time / rest time
2pm	Baby up, change and feed baby
3pm	Friend over for a cup of tea (already arranged)

Time	Activity
4pm	Tidy up while baby on play mat / wearing baby in a sling
5pm	Partner home – take over baby, make dinner
6pm	Rest
7pm	Baby bedtime, bath, feed
8pm	TV with partner
9pm	Start getting ready for bed

You'll note in the diary that the 'friend over for a cup of tea' has 'already arranged' next to it. This is because a mother struggling with her mental health is unlikely to feel able to organize an impromptu coffee date. A common mistake with these kinds of goals is assuming that writing it down is enough to be able to then follow through with it. Someone struggling with PND/PPD is more likely to avoid making that phone call. Making it as easy as possible for her to follow through, by pre-arranging these kinds of things is going to set her up for feeling like she has accomplished something in the day, rather than beating herself up for avoiding something.

"The point of the schedule is to encourage more activity and make things a little easier – if it all goes to pot, it doesn't matter!"

While it is really helpful to begin to schedule things, be mindful that babies don't really care about what we think our day should look like. The schedule might get thrown out of the water if the baby doesn't nap or if there is a huge nappy explosion. And that is OK! The point of the schedule is to encourage more activity and make things a little easier – if it all goes to pot, it doesn't matter! The point is not to get hung up about following it to a tee, but purely to begin encouraging your loved one to do a little more and have a little more control over her time. Reassure her that this is not an all-or-nothing approach. If one thing gets thrown out of the water, that's fine. She can problem-solve around it, carry on with the next task, or give herself permission to throw it out of the window and start again tomorrow.

GRADUAL CHANGES

For a mother struggling with PND/PPD, the idea of being left alone with a baby all day, or venturing out on a walk or to a baby group, probably feels like climbing Mount Everest without any prior training. Building this up slowly, to help your loved one build her confidence is a really helpful approach. Some of the strategies outlined in this chapter may not be immediately implementable, especially if you, as a partner, are working, or as a relative or friend you have limited times to visit. However, perhaps taking some time off, having flexible working hours or trying some strategies over a weekend could help.

Being home alone: If your loved one is struggling to be on her own with the baby, which might be especially relevant if you are finishing any leave you've had since the baby was born, it might be that you leave her alone for 30 minutes with the baby (or even 10 minutes if 30 minutes is too much) and build this up over the course of a few days, working toward her being on her own for a few hours at a time.

If you are already back at work and your loved one is struggling on her own, consider enlisting the support of a friend or relative. Can they be with her during the days, for a few hours? She can gradually spend longer periods of time on her own until she feels more confident.

Going out: Identify a short route that she can walk on her own with the baby, perhaps even going with her the first few times. When she is ready to venture out on her own, be on hand – do this on a day that you are at home or you can visit for a few hours. Reassure her that you are at home and will be there when she gets back or that you can be called on if she needs you. Again, build this up and identify places she would like to be able to go on her own so that she is motivated to engage. You might encourage her to arrange to meet a friend somewhere – a park or a coffee shop, so that she is not alone the entire time.

Baby groups: If your loved one is looking to attend a new baby group or activity, it will feel daunting for many reasons. Firstly, for someone struggling with PND/PPD, there's a good chance that going to a new environment and speaking to new people is utterly terrifying. You could support her by visiting the place she is looking to go to, without any pressure to go in. You could then go with her or arrange for a friend or family member to go with her the first couple of times. You might then go with her but wait outside while she attends herself. Even though this might be challenging with respect to work, enlisting more support will hopefully mean that someone is available to help. Building this up slowly and helping her to build her confidence in her surroundings and maybe even meeting some other mothers will increase her confidence in going it alone.

HELP FROM AFAR

You might be trying to support a loved one with PND/PPD from afar. Perhaps you are a best friend living abroad, or simply have to work a lot so you cannot be there much. You won't be able to support your loved one in a practical sense, however, you can support her emotionally. This will involve you staying in touch, even when she might not be engaging with you very much. You might send her cards or letters with notes of encouragement. You might text regularly to check in. Being further away does not make your support any less valuable and, in fact, sometimes the physical distance can actually help someone to open up given that there might be a little more objectivity to be had.

If you are at a physical distance, you may have not yet built a relationship with the baby, nor had any opportunity to witness mum and baby together. This could help your loved one to feel that you are completely on her side and that there is less pressure from you. The fact that your attention is not torn between her and the baby can be advantageous, and can help your loved one feel like you are someone just for her.

KEY POINTS TO REMEMBER

- Practical support can help to take the load off a mum struggling with PND/PPD; however, being proactive rather than waiting to be asked is important.
- Your loved one may refuse support, but be wary that this could be a symptom of her PND/PPD where she feels she 'should' be able to do it all.
- You can help her with getting more sleep, household chores and self-care (showers, food, etc.).
- You can help mum with baby – feeding, changing, taking baby out; however, be mindful if she is especially anxious

about letting anyone help, or disengaged from baby already.

- Make things as easy as possible for mum whether that be with self-care (running a bath or preparing food), or ensuring the cupboards are stocked.
- Support your loved one to build more routine in her day to balance rest and activity, but also to promote a sense of control over her day. Work on gradual changes to help her build her confidence over time.

The advice here is likely not new and exciting, but sometimes being more mindful of the basics can be very powerful, especially for a mother struggling with PND/PPD.

However, practical support alone is unlikely to be sufficient to support your loved one in her emotional wellbeing and recovery. So next, we look at the emotional and psychological support you can offer someone struggling with PND/PPD which will help on a deeper level.

CHAPTER 7

EMOTIONAL AND PSYCHOLOGICAL SUPPORT

This chapter offers you some simple strategies to support your loved one's emotional and psychological needs. You are not expected to take the role of a psychologist, but hopefully these tools will equip you to be there for your loved one, while also guiding her in the right direction for managing her difficulties.

Before taking a closer look at some specific support strategies that you can implement, it can help to have an understanding of the wider psychological mechanisms at play and the role of Cognitive Behavioural Therapy.

UNDERSTANDING THOUGHTS AND BEHAVIOUR

CBT is based on the idea that our thoughts, feelings, behaviour and physical sensations are all interrelated. CBT emphasizes the role of thoughts and behaviour in this cycle, as these are the only two aspects that we actually have any control over, which means that if we change these, we can change our emotional and physical wellbeing. Here is a visual representation of that cycle:

We might notice feeling a bit sad, anxious or irritable, or perhaps we notice a physical sensation, such as our heart racing. It may seem as if these feelings come from nowhere and it can be difficult to make sense of them. However, we can view our feelings as a 'gateway' to our thoughts and use that emotional experience to understand more about our thinking and behaviours. Let's break down each aspect of this cycle to give you a little more insight.

THOUGHTS

A recent study estimated that we have on average 6,200 thoughts per day, which is a lot of thinking! Many of these thoughts are 'self-talk' – thoughts to ourselves, often about ourselves – and I don't know about you, but my self-talk isn't always very helpful! The way in which we think can have a powerful impact on our emotions and, likewise, powerful emotions can generate powerful thoughts. Often, we don't even register the thoughts we are having – they run in the background like white noise; however, while our conscious mind doesn't always notice them, our subconscious mind does. When we experience particular types of thoughts, our body reacts to them and that can set off the vicious cycle. For example, if you think 'I'm a failure, I always get things wrong', then you're probably not going to feel good about yourself. In fact, you're probably going to feel really sad, anxious or unmotivated.

There are many reasons for the negative thoughts we experience – perhaps difficult childhood experiences, relationship issues, lack of confidence and low self-esteem, or perhaps as a response to traumatic situations. Given that we have over 6,000 thoughts a day, it is impossible to pay attention to them all, and so many of them pop into our head, impact on our emotions, and we are none the wiser. Within the CBT model, we describe these uncontrollable thoughts as NATs – Negative Automatic Thoughts.

"If we have never really been asked to question our thoughts, no matter how negative or irrational they might be, we just believe them and act out on them."

Some thoughts are noisier than others, and so while some fly under our radar, others go off like sirens in our heads, and we can feel like we can't escape them. More often than not, these kinds of thoughts are negative. We don't tend to get overly distracted or overwhelmed with how good life is. Instead, our brain focuses on thoughts of not being good enough or worries about the future. There's good reason for this, in that our brain thinks it's doing us a favour by alerting us to a possible threat, but actually all that happens is that we experience negative emotions as a result. If we are experiencing lots of negative thoughts about ourselves, the world or the future, it shapes how we feel and behave and can lead us to feeling trapped in a vicious cycle.

Because we typically don't pay much attention to our thinking, we tend to trust those thoughts. If we have never really been asked to question our thoughts, no matter how negative or irrational they might be, we just believe them and act out on them. So we can begin to see how unruly and powerful these thoughts can be because of how they impact directly on our feelings and behaviour.

NATs are one of the aspects of CBT that we are really looking to challenge. We are hoping to catch hold of those thoughts before they have a chance to impact on our mood; or notice the thoughts and their impact and work toward reframing the faulty thinking.

FEELINGS

Our feelings can be a gateway to our thoughts, but it works both ways – the way we think affects how we feel and the way we feel affects our thoughts. With the vicious cycle there isn't a starting point, and so our emotional experiences can shift the way we are thinking about things. For example, imagine the scenario of feeling stressed at work. You have lots of competing deadlines and a lot on your plate. It is understandable that you would feel anxious or stressed about this. But then let's think about how that anxiety and stress affects your thinking. Do your thoughts become more assertive and confident the more stressed you become? Probably not. In this scenario, you might begin to question whether you are going to manage everything. You might begin to experience NATs about your ability and competence. You might then be pretty hard on yourself for not 'doing better'.

"When we are feeling a particular way
– anxious or sad, for example – our brain
looks for evidence to justify the feelings."

So, how we feel can impact negatively on our thinking. Our brains are really clever, so when we are feeling a particular way – anxious or sad, for example – our brain looks for evidence to justify the feelings. It begins to sift through (via our thoughts and memories) the reasons for us feeling the way we do and, as a result, we begin to believe those thoughts all the more. And so, we begin to see the vicious cycle beginning to form, and the bi-directional impact our thoughts and feelings have on each other. Now we can't change our feelings by themselves, but by challenging the thoughts, we can start having some control over our internal experience.

PHYSICAL SENSATIONS

All these thoughts and feelings have an actual physiological reaction because emotions and thoughts are information that our bodies use to stay safe. If our brain thinks we are in danger, our body gets primed for action to get to safety. For example, if a lion walks into your living room, you'll be grateful for your heart rate increasing and the surge of adrenaline that will help you get the hell out of there quick smart. The problem is we don't often have lions walking into our living room, and yet we still respond to our emotions in similar ways. Our brains haven't worked out the difference between fear and danger; they respond to any perceived 'threat' physiologically as danger, which then has a knock-on effect, confirming to our brain that something is terribly wrong. As such, we can experience all sorts of physical sensations including palpitations, breathlessness, hyper-alertness, difficulties sleeping, upset stomach, etc.

But our emotions and thoughts also have an impact on us physically when we are not in threat mode. When we are experiencing lots of negative thoughts and feeling low, our energy levels decrease. We become lethargic and lack motivation. We might feel hungrier than usual, or less hungry than usual, and have difficulties sleeping.

When we experience the physical sensations linked to our thoughts and emotions, our brain uses these physical signals as evidence that something is wrong and uses it to react or justify the negative thinking … and so we can see this vicious cycle building momentum.

BEHAVIOUR

How we respond to what we think and feel both emotionally and physically is really important. When the lion walks into the living room, your thoughts, feelings and physical sensations prime you for running like the wind to get to safety, which is super-helpful. However, when we feel anxious, and think that others are judging us, we might experience physiological sensations such as blushing or palpitations, and our behaviour may be to avoid certain situations – e.g. going to a party or speaking up in a meeting at work. On the surface that makes sense – avoid the thing that scares you. However, what is the knock-on effect of that behaviour? Isolation? Rumination? Disengaging with things that usually bring you joy? The behaviour we engage in as a response to our thoughts and feelings can have a huge impact on this vicious cycle, as the behaviour in turn further impacts how we think about a situation and, ultimately, how we feel about a situation.

"We avoid the things that make us feel anxious, but by avoiding them we never have the opportunity to overcome the anxiety."

Avoidance behaviour can be particularly problematic. We avoid the things that make us feel anxious, but by avoiding them we never have the opportunity to overcome the anxiety. We begin to disengage with our usual daily interactions and activities, and, unfortunately, the less that we do, the less we want to do.

PUTTING IT ALL TOGETHER

Let's consider then how this might look for your loved one struggling with PND/PPD. A typical situation might be that your loved one is struggling to bond with her baby, and is avoiding caring for the baby.

Thoughts
I'm a terrible mum. I am a failure.
I can't cope.
I'm just getting everything wrong.
I should be able to do this.
He's better off without me.

Physical Sensations
Crying
Numbness
Fatigue
No energy

Feelings
Depression
Guilt
Anxiety
Overwhelm

Behaviour
Avoids feeding baby.
Doesn't respond or hand baby over to someone else when the baby gets distressed.
Avoids looking at baby or interacting with them.
Stays in bed all day.

As you can see, the way in which your loved one's thoughts, feelings, behaviour and physical sensations interact with each other can really heighten the emotional experience in any given situation.

CBT places an emphasis on the thoughts and the behaviours when it comes to facilitating change and improving someone's mood. In this example, it might be that we try to challenge some of the NATs by looking at alternative ways of thinking about the situation; or we might try to address some of the behaviours, including some of the avoidance behaviours by considering the impact these have on the overall situation. If you were to help your loved one engage more with baby or promoted more routine, you might see some behavioural change – more time spent with baby, less guilt and more confidence in her ability to mother her baby. By changing one aspect of the cycle, we can promote change across the rest of the dimensions.

Having a good understanding of this CBT cycle is helpful when thinking about how we might begin to support someone with PND/PPD. If we can begin to understand some of our loved one's experience in this way, we can begin to see areas where we might be able to intervene and support change. It might be in seeing some behaviours that are contributing to the problem, or it might be in challenging some of the thoughts.

So let's move on to look at some specific ways you can begin to support your loved one's emotional and psychological wellbeing.

PROMOTING NORMALIZATION

The first step in providing emotional and psychological support is to normalize your loved one's experience, having gained knowledge and understanding of what PND/PPD is and how it can impact new mothers. With this new-found knowledge, you are perfectly placed to begin to normalize the experiences that will feel frightening and anything but normal for your loved one. Being able to talk her through her symptoms, and beginning to give them a label or context, will be the first step in helping her to acknowledge that she might be struggling, but also begin to shift away from her assuming it's her fault and toward some further help. Sharing some of the insights you've learned, empathizing with her experience, while also letting her know that lots of other women feel the same way, can begin to normalize this for her.

"You are perfectly placed to begin to normalize the experiences that will feel frightening and anything but normal for your loved one."

SELF-HELP STRATEGIES

There are thousands of self-help resources and strategies for managing mental health. These can range from really useful, to really not. The strategies outlined here are tailored specifically to help you help your loved one who is struggling with PND/PPD. Some of these she can hopefully begin to engage in herself with your help and guidance, while others might be little tools you use in the moment.

Let's have a look at some of the CBT strategies that you might be able to implement.

CHALLENGING HER THOUGHTS

You know that your loved one is experiencing an onslaught of negative thoughts about herself. These might be:

- 'I'm not doing this right.'
- 'I'm a terrible mum.'
- 'I'm a failure.'
- 'This will never get better.'
- 'I should be able to cope; I shouldn't be feeling this way.'

She will also no doubt experience a range of common thinking errors, which seem believable in her mind, but can be very skewed or biased. Some of the common thinking errors include:

- **All-or-nothing thinking:** Also known as black and white thinking, where there is only good or bad; success or failure, with nothing in between, e.g. 'I'm doing *everything* wrong'; '*Everything* is a disaster'; 'I'm a *complete* failure.'

- **Jumping to conclusions:** As humans we tend to think that we are really good mind readers, but the reality is that we're really pretty rubbish at this. An example might be, 'The midwife thinks I'm a terrible mum' or 'That other mum has it all together, she must think I'm useless.'
- **Over-generalizing:** Where one incident is used to predict all other situations, usually negatively, e.g. 'I couldn't get her to stop crying, I can't ever soothe her' or when a woman is struggling with breastfeeding in the first few days – 'I'll never be able to do this.'
- **Should and must:** Where there are fixed rules about how they should be, and what they must be doing, e.g. 'I should be able to do this without help'; 'I should know what I'm doing'; 'I should be able to soothe her'; 'I must do it all myself'; 'I must look like I'm coping.' Often these kinds of thoughts are pretty far away from how someone is actually feeling, but the rules get in the way of being able to do something differently – e.g. ask for help.
- **Emotional reasoning:** Where emotions are seen as facts, e.g. feeling guilty = 'I'm letting my baby down'; feeling lonely = 'No one cares about me'; Feeling overwhelmed or anxious = 'I can't cope with my baby.'
- **Dismissing the positives:** A mother struggling with her mental health will regularly focus on the things that didn't go well or that felt too much and discount all the good that

she is doing, e.g. 'I keep getting this wrong' rather than 'I found that feed difficult, but I've managed all the others.'

- **Labelling:** Where a negative label is applied to someone or something, e.g. 'I'm stupid'; 'I'm useless'; 'I'm incompetent.'

- **Personalization:** Where people blame themselves, or assume that things are personal to them, e.g. 'My baby keeps crying, she hates me / I'm a terrible mum / I've done something wrong.'

"Asking what she might say if a friend was struggling or thinking the way she is can help her to step outside of her experience and look at a more balanced picture."

When you notice your loved one expressing these thoughts or when you think she might be experiencing them without voicing them, you can begin to challenge them. Remember that your loved one believes these thoughts, and without being prompted to consider another point of view, she will likely continue believing them. Some strategies you can use to help begin to challenge these thoughts include:

- **Looking at the evidence:** Identify evidence to the contrary to the thoughts your loved one is experiencing. If she believes that she's 'not doing it right', start identifying with her all the things she's doing really well. When she believes that she is worthless, tell her why she is so very worthy. It's not about proving her wrong or being dismissive of her experience, but rather helping her to see the bigger picture. It's important to ask your loved one to engage in this process too – ask her to look for the contradicting evidence. This way you are doing more than reassuring her, which she may not believe in the first instance.

- **Challenge the 'shoulds':** Those rules that we have can be very difficult to free ourselves from, and your loved one is probably very invested in them given the stakes are so high. But if you can gently challenge them, it might promote a bit of flexibility in her thinking so that she can reduce the pressure she is placing on herself. When she says, 'I should be able to cope,' or 'I should know how to do this,' offering a reassuring, and more realistic perspective, can be helpful – 'How can you know how to do something that you've never done before? You are learning and doing a great job.'

- **Point out the positives:** Your loved one will be screening all her experiences, along with how her baby behaves and how others behave around her, looking for the negatives to confirm her beliefs about herself. Being proactive in pointing out the positives will help create some balance to the picture.

- **What would you say to a friend?** It's amazing how we can tap into our inner knowing and wisdom when we don't put ourselves in the middle of the picture. Asking your loved one what she might say if a friend was struggling or thinking the way she is can help her to step outside of her experience and look at a more balanced picture.

- **Thoughts aren't facts (nor are feelings):** So what are the facts? Being able to challenge your loved one's thoughts really hangs on this premise that thoughts are not facts. Yes, we might believe our thoughts, but that still doesn't make them true. We can believe a whole host of things – 'The sky is green with pink spots' or '1 + 1 = 5' – believing something doesn't make it true. Being able to hear your loved one's negative thoughts, knowing that she likely believes them, but being able to offer up a more realistic and balanced thought can be helpful. The same is true for emotions. Experiencing mum guilt is unfortunately an occupational hazard of motherhood, but often the guilt is not based on fact. Feeling guilty and being guilty are two very different things, and it could be helpful to remind your loved one of this when she is struggling.

WRITING THINGS DOWN

One of the most effective strategies for beginning to manage mental health difficulties is writing things down. There are a variety of reasons why this can be helpful; firstly, it helps to simply get it out of your head. When we sit alone with our difficult experiences, they can often feel a lot bigger and more complicated than they actually are. They can become intertwined with other things and can rattle around like a washing machine. Our thoughts move so fast, and so before we've finished a thought, we're on to the next one. It makes challenging our thoughts really difficult. Writing things down slows down the thinking, and usually we realize there isn't quite as much in there, or it's not quite as big as we thought it was.

Secondly, writing things down often helps to get a little distance and gain perspective. We gain a bit of objectivity when we see those thoughts in black and white on paper. Suddenly, what we thought was true and absolute in our minds isn't quite so clear-cut. It can also help us begin to see solutions to the problems we couldn't move past in our mind. When we write down a worry or a belief, our brain can't help but counter it – starting to write down these opposing beliefs can be really helpful to gain more balance and flexibility in our thinking.

"Starting to write down these opposing beliefs can be really helpful to gain more balance and flexibility in our thinking."

Thirdly, writing things down might make it easier for your loved one to communicate with those around her. Finding the words and the voice to be able to talk to someone about how she is feeling can feel too much for a mother struggling with PND/PPD. However, being able to take her time, free of interruption and without fear of reactions can be an effective way to begin expressing herself.

There are a variety of different ways to begin writing down and challenging your thoughts; there is no right or wrong way. It can be enough to just provide your loved one with a journal and pen, or she might prefer something a little more structured to begin working through her thoughts herself. Finding something that works for your loved one is more important than following any particular structure. However, if she might benefit from something a little more structured, below are a couple of diary formats that she can use.

A–B–C

The ABC strategy can be helpful to begin noticing the negative beliefs and the impact these have on our emotions and behaviours.

Activating Event	Beliefs/Thoughts	Consequences
• What's happening? • What is the trigger?	• Thinking errors? • Negative thoughts?	• Feelings • Behaviour

Help your loved one to complete the cycle as it is with all the negative thoughts and feelings associated with them. Then help her work through the second cycle, replacing the negative thought with a more balanced, realistic and helpful thought. Here are some examples:

Activating Event	Beliefs/Thoughts	Consequences
Baby won't stop crying, mum gets upset, dad takes over with baby.	I'm a terrible mum. I can't even soothe my baby. I'm such a failure.	• Sadness, anxiety • Distance self from baby • Avoids being left alone with baby

A more helpful perspective on this would be:

Activating Event	Beliefs/Thoughts	Consequences
Baby won't stop crying, mum gets upset, dad takes over with baby.	I need a break. I've been soothing her all day. I have settled her many times before.	• Anxiety reduces • Reassure self • Take a break • Calm down

LOG 'THINKING ERRORS'

Beginning to log the negative thoughts and their impact can be helpful to then beginning to problem-solve and challenge any 'thinking errors' (see page 133). Think about a difficult situation your loved one has experienced recently. Explore the sorts of thoughts she had about it, how she felt and what she did. In being able to identify these patterns, it gives both of you an opportunity to challenge her thoughts. Encouraging her to come up with a more helpful way of looking at the situation will lead her to balance out her thinking and ultimately how she feels. This strategy really helps to challenge that idea of 'thoughts are facts' that we've spoken about previously. Here's an example to give you the idea:

Situation	Unhelpful Thoughts	Feelings	Behaviour	Alternative/ More Helpful Thought
Forgot about a doctor's appointment	I'm so useless. They will think I'm a terrible mum. They are going to call a social worker. I'm a total failure.	Anxious; depressed	Avoid the doctor's phone call. Ask partner to take baby to the doctor. Withdraw and don't tell anyone.	Forgetting a doctor's appointment is understandable – I'm totally sleep deprived and a bit all over the place. They will understand.

EVIDENCE ANALYSIS

This tool can help your loved one begin to examine the evidence and look for the positives that she might be dismissing. The hope here is that while there might be some 'evidence' for the unhelpful thought, by looking for evidence against the unhelpful thought, many of those things will be discounted.

Situation/Unhelpful Thought: I can't cope with motherhood	
Evidence For	**Evidence Against**
I'm finding feeding hard	My baby is fed and is not hungry
I'm crying a lot	I look after my baby's basic needs
I get stressed	She is fed, clean and sleeping
I couldn't soothe baby	She is gaining weight
I'm not enjoying this	I can soothe her sometimes
The house is a mess	I'm not crying all the time
	Sometimes I enjoy it – like when we go out on walks
	I love my baby
	The main chores are done
	My baby seems content
	My baby is healthy
	My baby is well cared for
	I am managing to get us both up and dressed
	We are managing to get out a bit more

PROBLEM-SOLVING

Your loved one may find it difficult to see past an obstacle thrown in her way, whether that is because she feels totally overwhelmed, or because an obstacle confirms her belief that she is useless; these obstacles have a high chance of getting in the way of her engaging in meaningful/enjoyable/productive activity. Helping her to problem-solve will support her in being able to overcome these inevitable obstacles. Look out for potential problems:

- If she is going out and the baby needs feeding, is there somewhere she will be able to stop? Is there a toilet on route?
- Will she require public transport, or will there be parking?
- Does she know how to confidently put the pram up and down and secure the car seat?
- Is the changing bag well stocked and organized?

Anticipating problems in advance and coming up with solutions will help her feel more prepared and confident to manage anything that might come up and knock her off course.

CHALLENGING AVOIDANCE AND WITHDRAWAL

As we know, one of the symptoms of PND/PPD is avoidance and withdrawal from people or activities. Your loved one may struggle to contact a friend to meet up for a coffee, or to ask her mother to come and sit with her in the afternoons. The more she avoids making these kinds of contacts, the harder it will become. So, help her out. You could message her friend or mother and ask them to offer their support. You might ask your loved one if they would like you to ask for them. You might just offer her some support while prompting her to make the contact herself, sitting with her while she composes the text message.

If your loved one is avoiding going out, exploring with her what she is anxious about will be helpful. The more she can express her fears, the more likely it is that you can work together to overcome them. Help her set small, achievable goals, and then help her figure out how to work up to these.

The most important thing is that you keep challenging the avoidance and withdrawal. If you ignore it, then this will maintain the problem. Remember that the more she avoids and withdraws, the harder it will be to come back from that. Keep encouraging her to contact people and setting those small goals. Normalizing her experiences and empathizing with her, while also reassuring her that she can do it and is doing a great job will go a long way. You can also use the ideas above on building it up and problem-solving to help mum feel more confident in managing this.

"The more she can express her fears, the more likely it is that you can work together to overcome them."

DISTRACTION

When used appropriately distraction strategies can be very effective for helping reduce distress and then engaging in problem-solving, especially if your loved one is getting really overwhelmed and anxious. Our brains are very clever, and yet they struggle to pay attention to more than one thing at a time. Imagine it is like a radio – we can only really tune into one station at a time. If we are in a heightened state of distress, then our brain assumes we must be in danger and begins to look for that threat (see page 128). However, when we focus our attention on something else (because we are not actually in danger), our body begins to relax as our brain gets the memo that things are maybe OK. Distraction strategies can help shift the focus away from the 'distress channel' long enough to help the body and threat system begin to calm down. Here are some easy to implement distraction strategies for helping in the moment:

- Counting back from 1,000 in increments of 6s.
- Breathing techniques – for example, 'box breathing'. Imagine you are drawing a box with your breath: breathe

in for a count of four, hold your breath for four, breathe out for four, hold your breath for four, before breathing in again and repeat.

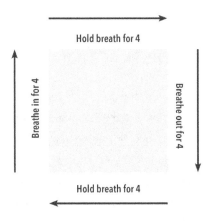

Hold breath for 4

Breathe in for 4

Breathe out for 4

Hold breath for 4

- Looking out of the window and noticing the colours of the trees, or the clouds in the sky.
- Counting all the letter 'T's on a page of a book.

You can see that many of these strategies involve quite a lot of mental energy – this is the point. We are distracting the brain away from that 'distress channel' long enough to help the body calm down. Once calm, we can then engage in some problem-solving around what triggered the anxiety in the first place.

Other more general distraction strategies for someone struggling with PND/PPD might be:

- Watching a funny movie
- Mindfulness
- Talking to someone else about what's going on for them
- Reading a book
- Painting/drawing
- Listening to a podcast or music
- Cooking
- Cleaning
- Social media

A NOTE ON SOCIAL MEDIA

While we all utilize social media to help distract us away from the stresses of life, it is important to recognize that there is also a flip side (and often darker side) to social media's impact on our wellbeing. Social media can be a wonderful place when we are in control of the content we are consuming and are mindful of how that content is making us feel. For women struggling with PND/PPD there are a huge number of motherhood bloggers and influencers on social media who have the potential to both help – or more importantly, hinder.

There are many 'perfect mother' accounts out there that depict only the best bits of motherhood. If these are the kinds of accounts your loved one is engaging with, the chances are she won't be making anything any better. We already know that a mother struggling with PND/PPD will be comparing herself against the world, and so these kinds of accounts are like falling into quicksand for a mother struggling with her mental health. Sit down with your loved one and consider the sort of content she is consuming. Ask her to think about how these accounts make her feel. If there are accounts that make her feel worse about herself or that she compares herself negatively against, encourage her to unfollow or mute those accounts. Instead, encourage her to highlight the accounts that make her feel empowered and less alone, and that normalize her experiences. There are a huge number of these types of accounts out there, but you may have to help your loved one more consciously search for these.

PROMOTING SELF-SOOTHING

You might be hearing a lot about 'self-soothing' with a new baby in the house, but no doubt this is directed toward the baby rather than mum. However, the ability to self-soothe is something that we could all do with getting a little more intentional about. It can be especially beneficial for a mother struggling with PND/PPD as she is likely to be hyper-critical of herself. She might be experiencing great deals of distress and anxiety, which she may or may not be able to express. Having tools to not only regulate those experiences, but to do so in a self-compassionate way, can be highly beneficial.

When we talk about self-soothing, we are talking about eliciting feelings of calmness and safety in the face of particularly distressing or overwhelming emotions. We are going for that feeling of 'Ahhhhh' as our shoulders drop, we release a breath we didn't know we were holding, and we feel utterly safe and at peace.

HOW TO HELP

Try this self-soothing exercise yourself, then encourage your loved one to try it too.

Take a moment to close your eyes and visualize a time when you felt completely safe. Imagine the place or the person where this feeling comes up most prominently. Begin to tap into your surroundings – what can you see, smell, taste, hear, touch? How do you feel? For me, it's being a little girl, and my gran stroking my hair and saying 'Aw pet' (very Scottish!) after I'd hurt myself. My gran always smells of fresh cotton and her house is always cosy and warm, and there's usually some chicken soup on its way if she's saying, 'Aw pet.'

You'll see from my example, and hopefully your own image that you've conjured up, that there is a focus on the senses. What can you see, smell, taste, hear and touch? Tapping into the five senses can be a quick and effective way of promoting self-soothing, as it taps into memories of the past (when we were safe) and away from the here and now. Smell is particularly effective for triggering that soothing sensation as it can go straight to the memory centre of the brain.

Identifying things using the five senses that promote that sense of safety and calmness is a great first step toward being better able to self-soothe and regulate those difficult emotions. Once identified, the next stage is to begin to collect those soothing strategies in one place, so that they can be implemented whenever needed.

THE SOOTHING BOX

Filling a box with objects that can trigger that soothing sensation can be a hugely self-soothing process in itself but, more importantly, having the box with everything together in one place means that it is easy to use, and there is little thinking involved. Having physical soothing strategies to hand can help your loved one begin to take back a bit of control over her distress, while also promoting a sense of calmness and safety, based on compassion.

Below are some suggestions for what you might include in the box, but the important thing is helping your loved one find what works for her.

Sight: She might include photographs of people or places that make her feel safe. It might be a particular object, piece of art or maybe even a video. I personally have always found water to be very soothing, and so images of sunset beaches or even videos of moving waves can feel very soothing for me. She might also include letters of support from yourself and others, or affirmations. It might also be a bit of poetry or writing that she loves.

Touch: Perhaps your loved one has a favourite blanket, jumper or a cosy pair of socks. Or perhaps a favourite type of fabric that she can hold, stroke or wrap herself in. She might also include things such as small objects like shells or stones that she can hold. It could even be a little reminder to ask for a hug, to cuddle the baby, to stroke the dog – or my personal favourite, to ask someone to brush my hair.

Taste: While it might not be practical to keep food in a box, it could be a favourite chocolate bar or sweet. Or it might be recipes for the soup her mum always used to make when she was little, or her favourite, hearty meal – one that soothes the soul. It could be things like peppermints, or a favourite kind of tea.

Sound: Ideas include notes and reminders for a playlist that your loved one has created on her phone – perhaps one that promotes calmness. It could be voice recordings from her favourite people, telling her she is doing great, or messages from her other children. White noise can also be effective – again, my favourite is the sound of rolling waves, I find it very soothing and relaxing and can almost tune out everything else. It could be a reminder to listen to some mindfulness or relaxation recordings. It's important that while the prompts are in the box, that your loved one also has a special folder or playlist or apps specifically for these soothing sounds so that it is accessible to her in times of need.

Smell: Remember that smell is particularly effective, so this is one to really think about. Often our favourite scents aren't always easily captured – e.g. the smell of freshly washed bed sheets, but it might be a prompt in the box to change the bedsheets or buy a particular fabric softener in a scent your loved one likes. I have 'Fresh Cotton' candles that I burn when I'm feeling a bit overwhelmed with life, as the scent takes me back to my gran. You could also burn essential oils. Placing a few drops of a particular perfume or aftershave on a bit of material in the box can also work. I always think that smell is especially useful given that you can have these scents around the home or carry them with you (on a tissue, for example). But it can mean getting a little creative. For the ocean – it might be some sea salt spray or a toiletries product that represents the scent. It can be quite fun going shopping and exploring different scents in the shampoo or candle aisle.

Once you have helped your loved one collate her soothing box, it is important to place it in a visible, easily accessible place (but out of reach of sticky fingers!). It might be on a shelf in the living room, or by her bedside table – somewhere she can access it, with ease, whenever she needs it. However, be mindful that your loved one might not always recognize when she needs the box, and so it can be a useful tool for you to be able to provide her with when you notice she's struggling. So, bringing through her favourite blanket, hot-water bottle and popping her playlist on for her can help to not only soothe her in the moment, but also make the connection to when she needs her box.

> "Having physical soothing strategies to hand can help your loved one begin to take back a bit of control over her distress."

Hopefully these tools will help you to feel a little more equipped to support your loved one who is struggling with PND/PPD, but remember that these are not intended to replace professional help and support. It is important not to take on all the responsibility for your loved one's wellbeing and to access the right help and support for her (see Chapter 10).

KEY POINTS TO REMEMBER

- Understanding the psychological mechanisms behind PND/PPD can give you an insight into your loved one's internal experience.
- Recognizing how your loved one's unhelpful thoughts and behaviours can impact on her wellbeing and her

relationship with her baby can help to identify areas that need to be challenged.

- Normalizing your loved one's experience is the first step in supporting her emotional and psychological wellbeing – if she is struggling with PND/PPD, she likely believes that there is something wrong with her, but does not know that it is a mental health issue.

- There are a variety of self-help strategies that you can implement with your loved one to help target those unhelpful thoughts and behaviours, including thought challenging, writing things down and problem-solving.

- Challenging withdrawal and avoidance behaviours is difficult but crucial to changing the PND/PPD cycle.

- There are various ways to support your loved one to regulate her emotional experience and promote more calmness, including distraction strategies and self-soothing.

Of course, PND/PPD affects not only your loved one's mood, but also their relationships with their baby and others. As humans, connection and good relationships are fundamental in good mental health, so promoting better connection with others will not only challenge these symptoms but will also work toward better mental health for your loved one. Next, we look at ways to build upon those key relationships in your loved one's life.

CHAPTER 8

PROMOTING CONNECTION

The more the PND/PPD takes over, the harder it will be for your loved one to make connection with others, whether that be with her partner, other children, her friends or family, other mums and perhaps, most importantly, her baby. She will find this difficult to do herself, because she will not feel deserving of it, or she will feel that she shouldn't need it; or she might just find it too overwhelming. Being able to help her build connections with those around her is going to be important in her recovery; and crucially, it's important to encourage your loved one's bond with baby.

BONDING WITH BABY

As we discussed in Chapter 2, your loved one's relationship and bond with her baby is likely to be one of the major difficulties if she is struggling with PND/PPD. And unfortunately, this difficulty has the potential to dramatically worsen the problem.

WHY IS BONDING IMPORTANT?

We know that there can be a significant and detrimental impact on a baby when they do not bond effectively with their mother, including developmental issues, attachment issues and even health issues. However, it is not only the baby that can be detrimentally impacted on by bonding difficulties. A mother who struggles to bond with her baby can be at risk of PND/PPD but also can be at risk of longer-term issues, e.g. parenting stress, along with longer-term mental health difficulties. So, bonding with baby not only is a symptom of PND/PPD but can also worsen PND/PPD.

In contrast, a positive bond with her baby will help mum produce oxytocin (also known as the 'love hormone'), which is shown to promote bonding and attachment, reduce stress and arouse feelings of calmness and love, as well as acting as a natural antidepressant. And the more oxytocin that is produced between a mother and baby, the more the mother will engage in behaviours that stimulate this hormone production. This is called a 'bio-behavioural feedback loop' – so the more a mother interacts and connects with her baby, the more she is driven to engage in interacting and connecting with her baby. As such, promoting a bond with her baby will help your loved one both in the short and long term in managing and recovering from her PND/PPD, but will also improve the overall health and wellbeing of both mother and baby.

BONDING DIFFICULTIES – WHAT TO LOOK OUT FOR

Many mothers struggling to bond with their baby will be acutely aware that something doesn't feel right – after all, bonding with baby is a primal and natural process; however, they may not express these feelings, and they may well mask it from other people – remember the shame that can be attached to this particular issue.

A mother struggling with PND/PPD may be avoiding her baby all together, or she may be overly preoccupied. However, at times, a mother struggling with bonding with her baby may mask this from other people, and on the face of it look as though she's doing just fine.

As well as the preoccupation or avoidance behaviours described in Chapter 2, a mother struggling to bond with her baby may also feel that her baby hates her or that no matter what she does, her baby doesn't respond to her the way they should. If she is struggling to bond with baby, your loved one may feel that she doesn't know what her baby needs at any given time; she may struggle to decipher a hungry cry from a windy cry, or she may not respond to her baby's cries at all. Your loved one is unlikely to be interacting with her baby above and beyond the essentials if she is struggling to bond, or may be very anxious about anything extra such as playing with her baby. She may avoid looking at her baby or even holding him or her; or if she does, she may appear uncomfortable and tense when doing so.

Knowing what to look out for can be useful in early identification of PND/PPD, given that not only can it be a symptom of the problem, but can also exacerbate the condition. If you can help your loved one bond with her baby early on, the effects of PND/PPD may be reduced.

HOW TO PROMOTE CONNECTION WITH BABY

Feeling disconnected from the baby can be one of the hardest aspects of PND/PPD. It is likely to cause feelings of guilt and shame, as well as adversely affecting your loved one's wellbeing. So gently supporting her to build that connection with the baby is crucial to her recovery and something to persevere with. Challenging your loved one's avoidance of the baby and creating opportunities for calm and relaxed closeness is key, but doing this in a gentle and non-judgemental way is important. If your loved one is getting distressed and overwhelmed, it is OK to step in and help, but don't whisk the baby away. Stay close and offer the baby back when she is a little more relaxed. Encouraging lots of eye contact and physical touch and interaction will help mum to understand her baby more, along with helping to stimulate oxytocin.

"Gently encouraging her to build that connection with the baby is crucial to her recovery and something to persevere with."

BABYCARE

Encourage your loved one to hold the baby when he or she is sleeping and content, when there will be the least amount of pressure and the most amount of enjoyment. She may need lots of encouragement, depending on how disconnected she is feeling. You may need to push it a little if she is avoiding the baby, but always be there to support her. Beyond this, give her the opportunities to feed, bath and dress the baby. Support her when this is challenging, but if bonding is seemingly difficult, providing lots of encouragement and support for your loved one to carry out these activities is important. Perhaps help her with bath time, and encourage her to wash baby and then wrap them up in a towel and have a cuddle while you clean up and sort out clothes, etc.; when changing a nappy, ask mum to talk to baby and play with baby while you sort out the messy business. Creating opportunities for mum to care for her baby will not only promote those bonding hormones, but will also build her confidence.

SKIN-TO-SKIN CONTACT

Skin-to-skin contact, where the baby's bare skin touches the mother's bare skin, is an excellent way of promoting the release of oxytocin. As well as encouraging interaction, it can calm and relax both mother and baby, and can even help to soothe an unsettled baby. It is also effective for promoting breastfeeding. Helping your loved one to create opportunities for skin-to-skin contact and encouraging her to do so will help to build this connection with the baby. If necessary, crank up the heating and provide a blanket so mum and baby can get cosy on the sofa for some skin-to-skin cuddles, or they could have a bath together.

BABY-WEARING

Rather than baby being placed in a pram or bouncy seat, wearing a baby carrier can help to stimulate that close bond and attachment. Again, your loved one might need some encouragement (and confidence) to carry her baby, but this can be an effective way to build closeness, again without too much pressure. This can be done in and around the house or when they are out and about. The more closeness between mum and baby, the better.

UNDERSTANDING BABY

Your loved one may be struggling to identify what her baby needs or wants if she is struggling to bond. Helping her to understand her baby's language can build her confidence and intuition about what her baby needs. If you notice this is something your loved one is struggling with, perhaps you can label the baby's needs in a gentle way while encouraging mum to respond to it. So if baby is crying and it sounds like they have wind (a high pitched, sore sounding cry), label it as "oh, looks like baby has wind" and then hand baby to her.

ACTIVITIES

Other things that can help to promote bonding include baby massage – your loved one doesn't need to go to a class; there are plenty of YouTube tutorials. Physically touching and talking to the baby can be really enriching for both mother and baby. If mum is struggling with this, do it together. Talk mum and baby through what you are doing, comment on the softness of baby's skin, or the way they smile when their tummy is being stroked. By modelling this kind of interaction with your loved one close by, she is more likely to feel able to engage and to notice little things like those long eyelashes or fuzzy little eyebrows when she is not in the grips of the PND/PPD.

Reading, talking and singing to the baby can also promote bonding. A mother struggling with PND/PPD might find these kinds of activities overwhelming or daunting, or may appear to have no energy or interest in them. You can support her by asking her to join in with you when you are singing or reading to baby. You could also invite her into the 'conversation' you are having with baby, e.g. 'What do you think of this silly face, mama?' Being sure to include your loved one in your interactions with baby will provide her more opportunity to learn what her baby likes, and build her confidence in trying it out herself.

Playing games with baby can also promote connection. Whether it is a game of peekaboo, getting down on the floor for tummy time or playing with some sensory toys, play can be a wonderful gateway to connection and bonding. A baby's laugh and smile is contagious, and so seeing how their baby responds to and enjoys these activities can help mum on both the physical and emotional level.

"I vividly remember the health visitor telling me to study my baby's face to help me bond with her – to notice her little eyebrows and eyelashes; to look at her fingernails and her toes. I remember thinking that this was stupid and a bit pointless, because every time I looked at her, I just wanted to cry – so how could looking at her this closely help anything? But then one night I was holding her, as she slept, and I noticed the shape of her eyebrows for the first time and it felt like something flicked on inside.

It wasn't a huge rush of love but it did spark something in me, that before that point had just felt numb."
Jenna

"At the beginning, it felt as though if I were a robot, the baby wouldn't care – I was only good for producing milk, there was no feeling or affection. But when he started to smile and laugh I finally started to feel as though I was getting something back. Those early days and weeks feel relentless but suddenly he was able to start interacting with me which made it feel easier to interact with him."
Stefania

PARTNERS

The most important thing you can do, as a partner, in promoting connection is not seeing these changes and challenges as personal. Your loved one's mood is what is most likely impacting on her relationship with you and so recognizing that it is not necessarily her choice is important. This will help you from reacting to her withdrawal or avoidance with your own anxiety and frustration. Seeing these changes as temporary, within the context of PND/PPD, will allow you a little more room for patience and understanding, while also not panicking that your relationship is breaking down.

Try to spend some time alone with your loved one – turn off the TV and talk to each other. Giving her your close attention might help her to feel more able to open up. You might ask someone else to take the baby for an hour while you spend some time together. You don't necessarily have to push her to talk, but rather just being there with her can help her feel safer to begin to communicate a little more. You could even think of ways of making it fun – playing a game or talking about funny events from the past. Anything that can remind your loved one that you are there for her.

Physical contact can be powerful; however, a woman struggling with PND/PPD may push away any affection, and is very unlikely to be interested in sex. This can be for a variety of reasons, from feeling unworthy, or that the affection may make her feel more vulnerable (that whole, when someone is nice to you, it's more likely to make you cry); or it may be that her PND/PPD is affecting her sex drive (although this is also true without PND/PPD following childbirth), or her confidence in her body may be affected – again either by the PND/PPD or by the changes following carrying a baby.

Be sensitive to your loved one's needs and boundaries. You might offer her a hug, or simply hold her hand when she's having a difficult time, or maybe just sitting close by on the same sofa is enough. Most importantly though, it's not letting her push you away too much, or rather not letting yourself feel pushed away. She might try to do this, and it can hurt, but continuing to show up, even when she doesn't necessarily want you there, will keep reminding her that she is not alone in this. We will discuss in more detail how you can look after yourself with some advice on how you can manage this difficult experience later in Chapter 9.

FRIENDS AND FAMILY

Maintaining a good relationship with your loved one when she is struggling with PND/PPD might be especially difficult from afar. Make sure that you maintain contact. Call her. Visit her. Stay in touch with her and remind her that you are there for her. It is going to be creating opportunities to spend time together that will promote that connection. Don't wait for your loved one to reach out to you, that may feel impossible for her; instead reach out consistently. Don't allow yourself to be pushed away. And if she doesn't feel able to connect with you, let her know that you are there for her whenever she is ready.

CONNECTION WITH OTHER CHILDREN

One of the most painful and difficult relationship issues that may arise from PND/PPD is your loved one's relationship with her other children. You may notice that she is withdrawn and avoiding her other children and they won't understand why she is being quiet or not playing with them; they won't understand that she isn't really angry with them but is just feeling really sad; and they won't understand that it's not their fault. This adds a whole extra dimension of complexity for you, as not only are you trying to meet your loved one's needs, but also the needs of any other children. Additionally, the older children will also be going through a period of change, with a new baby brother or sister, which can be unsettling and cause some difficulties in their emotions. If their mummy is also struggling and pushing them away, this has the potential to be very problematic for everyone.

It is important to reassure the child(ren) that they are not the cause of mummy's behaviour, but also to reassure your loved one that her difficulties with her older children are not because she is a bad mum. Remember, she will be looking for any evidence to support her belief that she is a terrible mum, and this will apply to all her children – especially if she can see that her behaviour is upsetting her children but she feels powerless to change it.

So, encourage them to go for naps together or snuggle up and watch a film while you take care of baby. Try to put as little pressure on your loved one as possible, while still facilitating connection with her children. Avoid the big events like solo trips to the park or big outings. Instead, keep things relaxed, slow and natural. Bring the child to her if she is feeding the baby or has been withdrawn, and encourage cuddles and love. If she is appearing particularly overwhelmed, then it might be helpful to distract the child and give them plenty of cuddles and reassurance yourself, but continually keep trying to promote connection. Mealtimes and bedtimes can be a good way to promote connection without too much pressure. Simply encouraging your loved one to be around her family will be beneficial.

KEY POINTS TO REMEMBER

- PND/PPD is likely to make your loved one feel more disconnected from those around her; however, those connections are more important than ever at this time.
- Creating opportunities to build on and develop these connections will be helpful for your loved one, as she will likely feel unable to do this herself.
- The bond between mother and baby can have an impact on the health and wellbeing of both.
- A good bond can stimulate good health and wellbeing, as well as stimulate mum to seek more closeness with her baby.
- Difficulties with bonding can impact on the development of baby, but can also impact on the wellbeing of mum.

- PND/PPD can be exacerbated by these difficulties bonding, as well as the difficulties bonding being a symptom of PND/PPD.
- Encouraging eye contact, physical touch and talking to baby will help to stimulate oxytocin – 'the love hormone' which helps to promote attachment and bonding.
- Activities such as skin-to-skin, baby wearing, baby massage, reading and singing to baby can help to promote bonding.
- As her partner, try to create opportunities for quality time, but try not to take it too personally if she pushes you away initially. Be respectful and patient, but don't let yourself be pushed away.
- Promoting connection with your loved one's other children is also important. She may be finding it difficult dividing her attention, or her PND/PPD may cause her to feel that she is failing them as well as the baby, so create opportunities for this that are pressure free.
- Encouraging connections with her wider support network is important. Set up opportunities for her to engage with her friends and family; and as friends and family, take the initiative to connect with her.

While bonding with baby is not the only relationship that suffers at the hands of PND/PPD, it is perhaps one of the most difficult and important ones because of the power it has in either exacerbating or improving the difficulties caused by PND/PPD. Promoting a positive and close bond between mother and baby will not only help your loved one in her recovery, but will also benefit both mum and baby in the long term.

There will be many layers of challenges to promoting this bond, including how your loved one is thinking and feeling, but being conscious and proactive in supporting mum to build this close relationship is essential to her recovery.

There are other relationships that are important to promote connection in too, including with partners, family, friends and other children. The more support your loved one feels she has, the closer she will feel to others, and the more accepting she will be of this support. However, the impact of PND/PPD is not exclusive to mother and baby, and you may find that supporting your loved one through their PND/PPD has an impact on your own wellbeing. Next, we will look at how you can look after yourself as you look after your loved one.

CHAPTER 9

LOOKING AFTER YOURSELF

Watching your loved one struggle with PND/PPD can leave you feeling powerless and lost and will certainly have an impact on your wellbeing. Whether it is because you are worrying or because you are bearing the brunt of her big emotions, it can be very challenging. Depending on your relationship with your loved one, the impact on your own wellbeing will differ. As her partner, you are likely going to be the most affected, but that same sense of powerlessness and confusion applies if, for example, you are a mother watching your daughter struggling.

Acknowledging that you have needs too, and that these needs matter, is important, while also balancing trying to meet the needs of your loved one. I appreciate that much of what you have already read has emphasized your helping role, and it seems like a big job. But it cannot be a job that you do to the detriment of your own wellbeing, otherwise both of you will potentially end up in a dark place, and that's not helpful for anyone.

It really is true that you 'can't pour from an empty cup', and so it is important that you find ways to not only conserve some of your energy, but look at ways to fill that cup back up. While you might believe that you don't need to prioritize yourself, that your loved one is so much more important, if you only pour into her cup, you will soon find that you have nothing left to give. We often get caught in the trap of ignoring our own needs, because it somehow feels selfish. But self-care is not selfish; self-care is essential. So, in this chapter, we will look at ways to take care of your own wellbeing while also caring for your loved one. It is not an 'either/or' situation here; it is a 'both/and'.

"I just felt so powerless and like nothing I did was enough to make anything better. Work was busy and everything started really getting on top of me. I ended up totally burnt out and exhausted – it hadn't really occurred to me that I had to look after myself too. My partner just seemed more important."
Shane

IMPACT ON RELATIONSHIPS

There is little doubt that if your loved one is experiencing PND/PPD this will impact on your relationship. This is likely to manifest itself in several ways and will differ depending on the relationship you have with your loved one.

PARTNER

The relationship you had before the baby came along will have changed dramatically overnight. You will both have shifted your focus and priority on to the baby, which is how it should be, but that means your focus will move away from each other. If your loved one is struggling with PND/PPD, then she may become withdrawn and distanced, which creates a chasm of space between the two of you, and your attempts to close this distance might even get rejected or ignored. This distance can affect the simple day-to-day things like having someone to talk to, to share your day with, to lean on when you've had a hard day. Your loved one is unlikely to have the capacity to pay attention to how you are doing, which can leave you feeling isolated and lonely.

Alternatively, you might notice that your loved one is increasingly in need of your reassurance and that she struggles when you are not there. You might find that she is leaning on you much more than before, and this can feel overwhelming. The woman, who likely, up until this point, has been relatively independent, is relying on you for everything. This can end up feeling a bit suffocating and can lead you to start feeling anxious too. You might find yourself craving space, but not feeling able to get it due to her need of you. As such, you might find that you start distancing yourself unintentionally, which might create other problems in the relationship.

"We felt like strangers for a long time. I felt like I was walking on eggshells and couldn't do anything right. But as she began feeling better, she seemed to be more like herself and things improved."

Conor

These changes can also create difficulties with intimacy. Your partner may be feeling so overwhelmed that even a cuddle from you is too much. There is a high chance that she will withdraw from physical and sexual intimacy. This is normal after having a baby, but a mother struggling with PND/PPD will find this all the more difficult. She may appear completely disinterested and may outright reject you. And while we all have a huge amount of compassion for a woman feeling this way, that doesn't make this kind of behaviour any easier on you.

"You might find that she is leaning on you much more than before, and this can feel overwhelming."

Mental health difficulties can cause a huge strain on your relationship, but it is important for you to understand that these changes and challenges in your relationship are not necessarily a true reflection of your relationship. As things start to improve for your loved one, there will be opportunities to close the distance that has been created. What she is going through is temporary and so these difficulties in your relationship are also temporary (so long as she gets the right support). How you respond to those challenges is important (again, trying not to take it personally), but that doesn't mean it doesn't affect you, which is why knowing how to look after yourself as well during this time is so important.

"I had to keep reminding myself that she wasn't well, because otherwise I'd have thought she really didn't want me around during those early days."
Luke

FAMILY AND FRIENDS

As a friend or family member, you might experience your relationship with your loved one slightly differently. You might find that she is avoiding your calls or seems withdrawn and disinterested in your relationship. Again, you will likely notice a shift in the balance of your relationship, where previously this might have felt more equal.

You might also find that your loved one's behaviour toward you is unpredictable. She might be smiling and laughing with you one minute and be completely withdrawn the next. The main difficulty in this kind of relationship is that you might not be getting the whole story, and you might feel as though your loved one isn't being honest with you. It's important to remind yourself that this is unlikely to reflect your actual relationship, and is more a reflection and reaction to the difficulties she is experiencing.

PUSHING PEOPLE AWAY

Whatever your relationship with your loved one, you might notice that she tries to push you away. She might be really good at this, either saying that she doesn't need your support or that she doesn't want it. This is really hard to hear and can be damaging to relationships, but if you can create a bit of space between what she is saying/doing and recognizing that this is likely due to how she is feeling, it will be easier to not take it personally, and to also stand your ground. The more your loved one pushes you away, the more she probably needs you. Again, this isn't easy for you, and so caring for your own wellbeing in the face of these painful experiences is crucial.

"The more your loved one pushes you away, the more she probably needs you."

RESPONSIBILITY – WHAT'S YOURS AND WHAT'S NOT?

We have covered a lot in this book already about the fact that your loved one will need a lot from you – and possibly even need you to be a mind reader (no small task there!). It would be very easy for you to slip into the mode of feeling responsible for her, and while of course you are responsible for some things, you can't be totally responsible for her. Due to the PND/PPD, your loved one won't necessarily be taking responsibility for herself, and she will need help and a gentle shove in the right direction of seeking support, but ultimately you cannot do everything for her.

> "By acknowledging that you cannot carry it all, you will allow yourself to reach out to others and ask for the help that you both need."

This is a really difficult thing to sit with. It can leave you feeling even more powerless and lost, but recognizing that you cannot do it all is really important. No one person can meet all the needs of anyone else; let alone a mother with the complexity of needs she carries when struggling with her mental health.

This is where I come back to the idea of 'no man is an island', and by acknowledging that you cannot carry it all, you will allow yourself to reach out to others and ask for the help that you both need.

If you get caught up in believing that you are responsible for every time your loved one gets upset, then you might miss what is actually going on. Taking on all the responsibility prevents her from taking responsibility for her own wellbeing, and you both remain in the cycle of externalizing the problem. There may well be times when her frustration with you is justified, but this is just a word of caution about accepting the responsibility too readily. The more of the responsibility you take, the less your loved one takes.

"Remember, you cannot do the work for your loved one; you cannot make her better; you cannot fix the problem."

For example, you might find that you are having arguments and that she is easily upset. It might appear that you have done something wrong to provoke this reaction, but much of the time the emotional response – for example, to you not emptying the dishwasher – is disproportionate to the event. This is an indication of what is going on for *her* rather than you being the worst partner in the world for not emptying the dishwasher (again, try not to take it personally – but also, empty the dishwasher!).

> "My wife just kept getting really angry with me over the smallest things. I couldn't understand what I was doing wrong, but she would nit-pick at everything. Once I realized that she was struggling with PND/PPD, I realized that what I was doing (or not doing) wasn't really the problem. That meant I could start focusing on getting her some help rather than what I was doing wrong."
>
> James

Remember, you cannot do the work for your loved one; you cannot make her better; you cannot fix the problem. You can be loving and supportive, pick up the slack and push her toward the help she needs; but ultimately for her to begin to take steps toward feeling better, she needs to be the one to put the work in. This is incredibly hard when we are talking about a mother struggling with her mental health, because we have also said that it's too much to expect her to be able to do this herself. But that is where your love, support and help need to be focused toward getting her the right help, so that she can engage in that help – unfortunately, you cannot do it for her, and in trying to, not only do you run the risk of burning yourself out, but you also prevent her from doing it for herself.

SO, WHAT ARE YOU RESPONSIBLE FOR?

You are responsible for:

- YOUR wellbeing
- YOUR emotions
- YOUR behaviours
- YOUR reactions

You are likely to be feeling overwhelmed yourself from adapting to parenthood alongside caring for your loved one. You might begin to feel some of what your loved one is feeling because of the empathy and love you have for her or because it is also taking its toll on you. You might notice feelings of hopelessness and fear, which may be a result of what your loved one is experiencing, or it may be related to whatever else is going on in your life.

While a new baby is all-consuming, and worrying about your loved one is all-consuming, there are likely to be other difficult things going on in your life, whether it be work stress, your own mental health, etc. This stuff won't just get put on hold until your loved one is feeling better. Often, we are juggling many balls, and as we are not superhuman, things take their toll on us. Keeping an eye on the other life 'stuff' is important because, while there might not be a huge amount you can do inside the bubble, there are likely to be things you can do to make the issues outside of the bubble a little more contained. Being mindful of your own mood is crucial and being responsive to it is more important. Noticing when things are getting on top of you and acting on that is not only a very good set of life skills, but even more essential when you are caring for someone with PND/PPD.

Something else you might notice, and probably don't want to think about or admit to, is that you feel really frustrated and annoyed with the situation. You might notice yourself becoming less empathic and patient as time goes on and might even feel resentful that nothing seems to be changing. I know! I know! This sounds horrible, doesn't it?! I mean, imagine getting angry with your loved one for being depressed … but it happens … you are only human! You might be annoyed with the situation, or you might even be annoyed with your loved one. And that is OK! Those feelings are perfectly understandable and valid. It is important to acknowledge them, because in doing so you also have a choice in how you respond to them.

"Being mindful of your own mood is crucial and being responsive to it is more important."

If these emotions are left unchecked, then they end up affecting our behaviour – think back to the CBT cycle in Chapter 7 – how we think and feel impacts on what we do. If you are walking around feeling angry and resentful that nothing seems to be changing, there's a good chance you might end up being less patient; less understanding; less compassionate; and, ultimately, less available to your loved one. You might end up doing or saying something that you don't really mean, and this may have a detrimental impact on your loved one's already fragile state. Recognizing your own emotions allows you to make decisions about how to respond to them, so that you can put boundaries in place, seek additional support or simply have a chat with yourself to reframe some of your thinking *before* you react.

Again, this doesn't mean that you let everything go; there might be times when you have to assert your boundaries or remove yourself from the situation. But this relies on you taking responsibility for your own emotions and behaviours so that at least one of you is making choices about how you respond.

SELF-CARE

I'll say it again: self-care isn't selfish! We often live in a world where everyone else's needs come before our own, and if you are caring for a loved one struggling with PND/PPD, then your needs will be even further down the list. However, knowing how to look after yourself is critical to looking after someone else.

Self-care can come in many different forms, and there is no right or wrong way. Of course, you might be somewhat limited in what you can engage in – long weekends away and big nights out might not be the most appropriate options after the arrival of a new baby; and long lie-ins and early nights might seem like things of the past, so you might need to get creative. Below are some ideas for how you might factor in some self-care, so that you will be in a better position to look after your loved on.

SLEEP

While sleep deprivation is part and parcel of having a new baby, it is important that you are still trying to get as much rest as possible, especially when you are also caring for your loved one. It is easy to fall into the pattern of helping your loved one get her own rest and foregoing your own. This might work for a while, but is certainly not a sustainable option. It might be that you try to take things in shifts, if she is feeling up to that. You might stay up late, and get up early, but get a few solid hours through the night while your loved one takes over feeding duties. This divide and conquer approach to the sleepless nights can benefit you both – ensuring that you both get at least a few solid hours of sleep each night, even if it is still not quite enough.

It might be that you need to factor in a daytime nap or you might need to call granny to come for a couple of hours so you and your loved one can both get a break. Finding ways to get some shut eye is a central point in self-care and will benefit everyone. When people say 'sleep when the baby sleeps', new parents often roll their eyes, because when the baby sleeps the chores need to be done. However, in these circumstances, prioritizing sleep is more important. Yes, the washing might need to be done, or the dishes might need to be cleaned, but taking that hour to shut your eyes is going to be much more helpful … the washing and dishes will be there when you get up. And I say this with all seriousness – having been a new parent myself, and not taking this advice, I really wish I had taken the opportunity to sleep when the baby slept … at least some of the time!

Rest can be as good as sleep

OK, not really, but it is the next best thing! Regardless of how many opportunities you take to get some sleep, you will still be exhausted. So, as well as trying to prioritize sleep, try to get as much rest as you can. Rest, while definitely not the same as sleep, can help to keep your exhaustion levels down. It will be tricky, but finding those pockets of time to slow down will be hugely beneficial. Again, you might have to get creative. Here are some ideas:

- Opt for a takeaway or microwave meal instead of cooking.
- Take a midweek annual leave day.
- Take a book on your walk with the pram and take some time to sit in the park and read rather than walking for miles.

- Say no to visitors – or better yet, say yes and then let them make you the coffee or do the dishes.
- Accept offers of help with the baby, then rather than filling that time with the 'to-do' list, sleep or sit on the sofa and watch some rubbish TV.

"To get some rest I would walk my daughter to the park at nap time and just sit on a bench for an hour. Sometimes I'd read, other times I'd sit and eat my lunch. I'd realized that I was spending the whole of nap time walking around and around which was killing me!"
Jake

EATING

I know it sounds incredibly basic but as you are reading this, have a think – what have you eaten and drank today? You might be sitting reading this during nap time and have only had one or two (dozen) coffees so far. Or you might be reading this before you head off to sleep and realize that you've only had one out of three meals. We often forget about nourishing ourselves when we are looking after someone else. You might be making sure your loved one and the baby are fed, while completely ignoring your own thirst or rumbling stomach, thinking that you'll get yourself something later (and later never comes).

So rather than making your loved one a sandwich and thinking you'll make yours later, make yourself something at the same time. Take a sandwich with you or stop by the coffee shop on your walk with baby to grab some lunch. When you are at the supermarket, add in a few extras that you can grab on the go – breakfast bars, pre-prepared fruit, microwave meals, ready meals, pasta pots, sandwiches – anything that is quick and easy for you to grab. You might also think about batch-cooking some evening meals – chilli, bolognese, casseroles, etc. Or better yet, ask someone else to do this for you and stock up the freezer!

DON'T FORGET THE EXTRAS

Find some time to exercise – not only does it produce those happy hormones, but it can also give you a much-needed energy boost. Even just going out for a walk in the fresh air is a good mood booster.

Find small pockets of time to engage in your hobbies; it's so easy to let go of these entirely when a new baby comes along, but even half an hour of reading, gardening, music or drawing is better than nothing.

REDUCE THE LOAD

We all carry our own expectations and standards in life, whether that be in our work, home or social life. However, right now, if you are caring for a loved one struggling with PND/PPD, being able to achieve everything you once did, to the standard you previously did, is impossible. A baby alone adds a huge additional load, but add in the care for your loved one, and you are carrying more than you've likely ever had to carry. So, lowering your standards and shedding the load is not only helpful, but probably necessary.

> "Being able to achieve everything you once did, to the standard you previously did, is impossible."

Accepting that the housework will slip; accepting that you'll probably have to let other people down by saying no more; accepting that your work performance won't be quite the usual standard – these will all help to reduce the load. Again, here you can let other people help. Sharing the load is an excellent way to reduce it.

WORK

Consider taking some time off work – whether it's a couple of days to extend the weekend or a couple of weeks to recharge. Trying to do it all, all the time, is a sure-fire way to burnout. It may be that you could work from home a couple of days a week to help out with baby and avoid the commute. Or perhaps you could discuss with work the option of cutting back a little.

Similarly, being able to reduce the load at work might be helpful. Saying no to the extra hours; delegating a little more; making a point of not bringing work home; not taking on the extra work; trusting that your 80 percent is good enough and holding back a little are all ways to ease the workload to give you a little more capacity at home.

YOUR EMOTIONAL WELLBEING

It is known that partners of women suffering from PND/PPD are at increased risk of developing depression, and so looking after your emotional wellbeing is crucial. Increased worry and anxiety are perfectly understandable and normal in these circumstances, but just because it is normal does not make it easy to tolerate.

Feelings of helplessness, along with the worry, exhaustion and your own struggles in adapting to parenthood can mean that you might need some additional support. Often, however, it is easy to dismiss your own experiences because your loved one 'has it worse' than you. This is dangerous, because if you do not attend to your own emotional wellbeing, there is a good chance you'll soon become unable to look after your loved one too. Noticing that your emotional wellbeing is suffering, or that your mood is deteriorating will help you address it much sooner, rather than stuffing it away in a box, only for it to explode somewhere later down the line.

Much of the advice already offered in terms of looking out for your loved one's symptoms of PND/PPD can be helpful for your own self-monitoring and knowing when to intervene. Acting in response to this is just as, if not more, important as responding to your loved one's mental health difficulties. If you notice your mood is deteriorating, talk to someone. Speak to a friend or family member – share the load. Prioritize your self-care. Take time off. And if these things don't help, ask for help for yourself. Talk to your own doctor or even the health visitor. While a lot of attention is focused on mum's mental health, your mental health is also important.

You can access a range of support services including counselling, medication or even support groups. Don't be afraid or ashamed to access these services. Remember that your wellbeing is fundamental for being able to look after your loved one. Don't wait too long to ask for this help. The longer you leave it, the harder it becomes, and the worse you and your loved one might end up.

"Being able to speak to my own therapist during those months was so helpful. It helped me work out what was my stuff and how I could help my wife. At first it felt selfish, but having that time to talk about my stuff helped me be there for her."

Andy

KEY POINTS TO REMEMBER

- Supporting a loved one through PND/PPD can have a significant impact on your own wellbeing – whether it be worry, relationship changes or bearing the brunt of her emotions.

- It is important that you acknowledge that you have needs too, and that you cannot 'pour from an empty cup'.

- PND/PPD may impact your relationship with your loved one. The support she was once able to offer you is no longer available; intimacy is affected; she may be pushing you away – it is difficult not to take this personally, but remember that it is PND/PPD rather than your loved one's choice.

- Pay attention to what you are taking responsibility for – you cannot fix everything, nor are you responsible for your loved one feeling the way she does. You can support your loved one, but you cannot make it all better for her.

- Take responsibility for your own wellbeing – notice and respond to your own emotions and needs; suppressing them will not help in the long run.

- Take time to engage in your own self-care. As hard as that can seem when your loved one is suffering, sleep, rest, food and exercise are important for you too.

- Reduce the load where you can – you cannot do it all, and if you do, you will burn out!

- Seek and engage with your own support systems – look for additional support for yourself too if you feel you need it.
- Self-care is not selfish – in the long run, the better you take care of yourself, the better you can support your loved one.

Now that you know a little more about PND/PPD, how to support your loved one and how to recognize the importance of your own wellbeing, let's move on to explore how you can get more help for you both.

CHAPTER 10

GETTING PROFESSIONAL HELP

This chapter provides you with guidance on navigating the different resources, to help you make an informed decision about where to access support. Before you jump into getting professional help, speak to your loved one about your concerns (see Chapter 5 for pointers on starting this conversation). Hopefully she will recognize that she would benefit from support and can be involved in accessing help. If, however, she is struggling to recognize that she needs support, there is advice in this chapter about how to begin that process yourself.

KNOW WHEN TO ASK FOR HELP

The ideal scenario is that your loved one feels able to contact these services herself, with your support. If she does, then the 'when' becomes pretty straightforward – straight away;

strike while the iron is hot! Support her to make the calls or appointments, but do it while she is motivated. Delaying it runs the risk of her retreating back into her shell. And although it is perfectly possible that things will improve with time, accessing support when she first seems motivated can do no harm. If it really comes to it and she doesn't feel like she needs ongoing support when she gets access to it, then she can change her mind at that point, but it is better to have the wheels in motion, rather than trying to restart them again.

> "Talking over your concerns with someone else will help you begin to make sense of what sort of support might be needed."

If your loved one is struggling to accept that she needs help and engage in support, then it might fall to you to make the decision of 'when'. Keep in mind that her resistance is likely a symptom of the PND/PPD rather than how she truly feels. Talking over your concerns with someone else will help you begin to make sense of what sort of support might be needed and validate your decision to make these calls yourself.

Again, remember that if you feel that your loved one is really not coping with their mental health and you are concerned about her immediate wellbeing and safety, you should call emergency services. It is always better to be safe than sorry, and better earlier than later.

KNOW WHO TO ASK FOR HELP

The first point of contact is usually the health visitor or GP in the UK or the family doctor or OB/GYN in the US. These healthcare professionals are well placed to consider the needs of both mother and baby, along with accessing more specialist support as necessary.

Often women can become fearful that if they disclose their mental health difficulties to a healthcare professional, they run the risk of losing their baby due to being seen as a terrible, incompetent mum, but this is very unlikely to happen. Healthcare professionals want to support a mother to look after her baby and her wellbeing independently, and so will ensure that she accesses the right support to facilitate this.

If you feel that your healthcare professionals are not taking your concerns seriously, then it is important to keep trying. Ask to speak to another doctor or health visitor. Don't take one person's dismissal as an indication that your concerns are not valid. Remember that you know your loved one better than anyone, and if you have concerns about her wellbeing, then it is likely that you are right.

Encouraging your loved one to speak with the healthcare professionals herself is the ideal way to access this support, but if she is unable or unwilling to do this, make that phone call yourself. Establishing contact with a healthcare professional is the first step toward accessing the right help. Supporting her to attend these appointments and encouraging her to be open with the healthcare professionals will allow them to make a proper assessment of her needs. Being there to support her each step of the way will help her to feel safe and supported.

KNOW WHAT TO ASK FOR

There are various treatment options available. Deciding which intervention is most appropriate will be a collaborative process between the health professionals, your loved one and most likely yourself. Options range from medication, to counselling, to psychological interventions, to the more extreme end of hospitalization (in the case of suicidality or psychosis). There are also community and peer support resources, along with more practical support from social work or the health-visiting team.

In most cases, your healthcare provider would make the initial assessment, looking at symptoms, daily functioning, mood and any risk factors. They may recommend medication with follow-up appointments or make a referral to more specialist services. Here is a brief overview of the sort of support that might be offered, but remember, there is no 'one size fits all' approach, and your loved one's preferences and needs will guide the process.

PSYCHOLOGICAL THERAPY

There is a great deal of evidence to support the use of psychological interventions for treating PND/PPD. Having a safe and confidential space, free of judgement, can be hugely beneficial for anyone struggling with mental health difficulties, but especially a woman struggling with PND/PPD and all the associated shame and guilt attached to it.

Psychological therapy comes in different shapes and sizes, and the type offered will depend on the healthcare you have access to, as well as your loved one's needs and preferences. Most often therapy will be for your loved one on her own, but there may be opportunities for you to join in with the sessions if appropriate.

Person Centred Counselling

Person Centred Counselling is a talking therapy that offers a safe space to explore difficulties and experiences, free of judgement or criticism. Your loved one will have plenty of space to talk through her own feelings, while the counsellor listens closely to her. The counsellor will provide lots of empathy and help your loved one to understand and process her difficult experiences and emotions. As counselling is a non-directive talking therapy, the counsellor will not typically offer advice or solutions; rather they will work with your loved one to find her own solutions to her difficulties. A strong therapeutic relationship built on trust and safety between client and therapist is at the core of this kind of therapy. It can be helpful for people who feel like they need space to talk and to be heard and understood, and who feel more able to lead the way when it comes to the sessions. It is suited to those who wish to explore and understand their difficulties rather than 'fix' them. The simplicity of being able to speak freely and to feel completely understood is very powerful, and counselling has a lot of evidence behind its efficacy.

Depending on the context in which the counselling is being offered, this work can be more open-ended than other therapies, meaning there isn't always a limit on the number of sessions offered. This can be helpful for people who like to work at their own pace. Counselling can often be accessed via charities and local health centres and is sometimes free or low cost. You can also access private, self-funded counselling, or counselling via any health insurance you might have.

Counselling is perhaps not quite so suited to people who are looking for practical or specific strategies for managing their mood. Counselling services tend to see individuals with mild to moderate mental health difficulties and would usually not see people who are at high risk to themselves or others – this would be more suited for psychological services.

There are other forms of counselling available, depending on the organization and practitioner, including integrative counselling (integrating a range of different approaches), gestalt counselling, and experiential/emotion-focused counselling. Therapists trained in different models of counselling may be able to offer more practical strategies, while still providing lots of space to talk through difficulties. Each practitioner will work in their own way, and so exploring their approach, either through their websites or in an initial conversation to see if it would suit your loved one's needs is advised.

"The simplicity of being able to speak freely and to feel completely understood is very powerful."

Cognitive Behavioural Therapy (CBT)

CBT is solution and problem focused, and therefore more suited for those looking to develop practical strategies for managing their emotional wellbeing. CBT focuses on identifying unhelpful thoughts and behaviours, which contribute to the difficulties an individual is experiencing, then uses a variety of different tools and strategies to challenge these thoughts and behaviours to help alleviate symptoms.

CBT has a very strong evidence base for working with mental health problems and is well suited for someone who is motivated to engage and make changes in their behaviour and thinking. It is quite a structured approach to therapy and can be time-limited depending on the context and the difficulty.

In CBT, the therapist will identify goals and an agenda for the session, and will follow a structured approach to this. The therapy is collaborative in nature, and so it is not a case of the therapist 'doing' anything to the client; rather the client and therapist work together to identify the goals. However, there is a focus on the client being active, and so there will be tasks set up in between sessions for the client to follow through with – sometimes referred to as homework. For someone struggling with PND/PPD, carrying out homework tasks may feel like an added burden. If your loved one does engage in CBT, it would be helpful to check in with her about any homework tasks that have been set, remind her gently and support her to carry these out.

This kind of therapy is perhaps not quite so suited to those who are looking for space to just talk through their difficulties. Sometimes people aren't looking for practical things to do, and just want someone to listen. This would not be what CBT would offer, and it might be that counselling would be more suitable for this kind of need.

A referral for CBT can be made by a doctor or through health insurance, but it is worth being aware that many services offer short-term CBT in the first instance. While this can be very beneficial for building tools and skills to manage mental health difficulties, there is less opportunity to explore difficulties in depth. You can access private CBT therapists if you are able to self-fund or have health insurance. CBT therapists are focused on working with mild to moderate mental health difficulties, and depending on the context and organization, they may not see individuals presenting with higher risk.

Clinical/Counselling Psychologists

Clinical/Counselling Psychologists are often trained in a variety of different models, including the ones highlighted above. The psychologist will carry out an initial assessment to discuss current symptoms and difficulties, take a background history and discuss aims of the therapy. From this assessment, the psychologist will tailor a psychological intervention plan. The type of therapy offered will vary depending on your loved one's needs and the psychologist's training. However, usually a mix of different approaches can be used.

Psychologists work in a variety of different settings from the health service to independent practice, and within charitable and voluntary services. Psychologists are highly trained and specialists in working with mental health difficulties, from mild to severe and enduring. They are usually more comfortable managing risk. Psychologists often work within Multi-Disciplinary

Teams (MDT), and so if your loved one requires input from other disciplines, such as psychiatry, nursing, social work or occupational therapy, they can often refer into these services and work collaboratively alongside the MDT staff.

In the UK, the demand for psychological services within the NHS is high and there can be a long waiting list. Being able to access more immediate support through counselling services or private practitioners can be an option, but this is something to discuss with your doctor.

PSYCHIATRY AND OTHER HEALTH PROFESSIONALS

A vast array of health professionals can offer support for PND/PPD, depending on individual needs. It might be psychiatry, nursing or social work – all have valid and useful support to offer. These services are grounded within a more medical approach to treatment, and so interventions will often include medication. These kinds of services can feel a bit intimidating, and people can feel worried about accessing this kind of support as it can feel more official than talking therapies. For someone struggling with PND/PPD, needing this kind of support may exacerbate her belief that she is not coping, or that someone is going to take her baby away because she is struggling. It is important to recognize that, while that can happen in some extreme cases, it is highly unlikely. In most cases, health professionals including psychiatrists and social workers, are looking to support someone through their mental health difficulties and are not there to judge – they certainly do not want to take a baby away from his or her mother, and this is an absolute last resort in *all* cases. These health professionals have their own skills and expertise, which can be invaluable in providing a woman with the care she needs, whether that is medication or more practical support at home.

PERINATAL MENTAL HEALTH SERVICES

These specialist services, which can be accessed during pregnancy and in the first year after the birth, focus on maternal mental health difficulties, and usually consist of a variety of disciplines, involving both out-patient and in-patient services, depending on the need. They are for women who are at increased risk and whose mental health difficulties are having a detrimental impact on themselves and their babies. As these are more specialist services, they are geared toward specifically working with maternal mental health-related conditions, but they can also be in high demand. There needs to be a referral from a doctor or private healthcare provider; once this happens a first appointment is usually made fairly quickly.

MEDICATION

Medication can be beneficial, especially in conjunction with therapeutic interventions. It can help with low mood, anxiety or mood stabilization, depending on the symptoms.

For a woman struggling with low mood, often a selective serotonin reabsorption inhibitor (SSRI) can be prescribed, which is a kind of antidepressant that helps to increase a hormone called serotonin in the brain. Serotonin contributes to feelings of happiness and wellbeing, as well as aiding sleep and appetite, which are all affected by depression and low mood. These are shown as very effective treatments for depression, and can also help with anxiety. There are also specific treatments for anxiety symptoms, including beta blockers, which help to regulate physical arousal levels that can trigger threat mode and feelings of anxiety.

While medications are shown to be very effective, they are not without their side-effects. SSRIs can take four to six weeks to begin to take effect, and can result in a number of physical and psychological side-effects. In some cases, SSRIs can exacerbate the mental health symptoms and so it is important that any medication is closely reviewed and monitored by a medical professional.

Medication and Breastfeeding

Some medications are not safe to be taken alongside breastfeeding. The doctor or psychiatrist will be able to advise on this, or they may wish to consult specialists in this area to ensure whether the medication they want to prescribe is safe.

However, it is also worth stating that there are many medications that are safe to take while breastfeeding and so requiring medication does not need to mean the end of a breastfeeding journey. In these cases, the prescriber will be balancing up the benefits to mum versus the risk to the baby. It is important that you and your loved one feel informed and supported in making a choice about medications and breastfeeding. So ask for clarification if there is anything you are unsure about. See Useful Resources for helpful websites on medication and breastfeeding.

SUPPORT GROUPS

There will be a number of other community-based support services that your loved one could access in your local area. These might include peer support services; parenting support groups; or charity and voluntary support services – either generic mental health or specifically for maternal mental health services. Your health centre, health visitor or family doctor should be able to provide you with details of such services available locally, and these will vary depending on your area. There is also a range of support services online, which may be beneficial, especially if your loved one is resistant to accessing formal support in the first instance.

HEALTHCARE PROVIDERS

If you believe that your loved one would benefit from seeing a psychologist or healthcare professional, including access to a psychiatrist or perinatal services, then the first point of contact for the most helpful conversations is your family doctor or health visitor. In the UK, your GP can refer you directly to any of the services required, while in the US your family doctor would refer to your private healthcare provider, and your access to these services will depend on your insurance cover, so it is well worth looking into this to see what might be available.

SELF-FUNDING

If you are able to self-fund, look online for an appropriately trained and accredited therapist. In the UK, a psychologist must be registered with the Health and Care Professions Council (HCPC), while the British Association for Counselling and Psychotherapy (BACP) and the British Association for Behavioural and Cognitive Psychotherapies (BABCP) register and accredit counsellors and CBT therapists. In the US, the American Psychological Association (APA) can guide you on finding a licensed professional.

KEY POINTS TO REMEMBER

- Accessing professional support can be an important step in your loved one's recovery but can feel daunting.
- Ideally, your loved one will initiate seeking this support herself; however, it may require some encouragement. Follow up any help-seeking behaviour quickly with suggestions. If you are worried about her and she is resistant to accessing this support herself, you may need to make contact on her behalf, with her permission.
- The types of support available will be dependent on healthcare cover and local services; discussing this with a healthcare professional in the first instance will guide you toward what is available.

Now you know where to look for additional support for your loved one, and can begin to make the necessary steps toward her recovery, let's look at what moving forward in your loved one's recovery might look like.

CHAPTER 11

MOVING FORWARD

I hope that by this point you are feeling more equipped to help your loved one access the support she needs. Once she begins to engage with that help, it is unlikely to be a quick, overnight fix. There is a journey of recovery ahead, and one that is rarely straightforward and smooth sailing, but remember that it can and does get better; it just doesn't necessarily happen quickly.

WHAT RECOVERY 'LOOKS' LIKE

Once your loved one begins engaging in further support, whether it's therapy, medication or the support you offer her, there will be weeks ahead of hard work, and ups and downs. She is likely to begin to slowly build her confidence, shift her thinking patterns and behaviour, and pull herself out of this dark place. However, it is not an all-or-nothing scenario. Her symptoms will not dramatically disappear and, in fact, may never go away entirely. She may still be struggling with low mood and anxiety for years to come, but having received help she will hopefully be equipped with the tools and resources to support herself. While she may still be experiencing symptoms, she will be much more equipped to function in spite of them, rather than experiencing the crushing overwhelm of postnatal/postpartum depression. It is important to manage your own expectations of this – be aware that there is no magic cure, and your loved one will not bounce back to the person she was before.

HOW LONG RECOVERY TAKES

How long is a piece of string? I know it's a cliché, but everyone's road to recovery is different. Your loved one might find her way out of PND/PPD fairly quickly with minimal input or support. Certainly, things can get easier the older the baby gets and the more your loved one regains her confidence. However, that is not always the case. As previously stated, medication can take about four to six weeks to take effect, so expect more weeks and months to work toward recovery. In terms of therapy, evidence suggests a minimum of 12–16 sessions of CBT is recommended for the treatment of depression, suggesting that improvement can be made in this time frame. However, it can take less or more time than this, and your loved one may only be offered a certain number of sessions.

> "It is important to manage your own expectations of this – be aware that there is no magic cure."

Some women recover in a few months, while others struggle for months, and sometimes years. Remember that early intervention is crucial so that the depression does not bleed into the years beyond early motherhood. It's also worth bearing in mind that depression (of any kind) is not a one-time only deal. Women can experience relapses in their mental health at any time, either within that first year of motherhood, or the years beyond. It is important to manage your own expectations of this. Thinking that your loved one 'should be better by now' might actually feed her anxiety and guilt at not being better already.

RELATIONSHIP WITH THE BABY

When it comes to her relationship with the baby, severe PND/PPD can be really damaging. Women may struggle with this for many years, despite the symptoms of depression diminishing. It is important to meet this with compassion and being free of judgement. If your loved one continues to experience these difficulties in her relationship with her child, she may struggle to voice it. By being compassionate, accessing support early on, and having your ongoing support, it is something she can continue to work on, and have the motherhood experience she deserves – it just might take more time and effort beyond the initial symptom reduction.

RELATIONSHIP WITH YOU

As a partner, not only has the PND/PPD had an impact, but you are also both adjusting to having a new baby in the family. It will take time to find your way back to each other, and to find time for each other again. It is entirely possible to maintain that healthy, strong, fulfilling relationship, but it is a process of months and maybe years – not days or weeks.

If you are a relative or friend, bear in mind the longer-term impact of PND/PPD and don't expect too much of your loved one too soon.

"It took me six months to be able to talk openly about what was going on, but then about another six months to start feeling more like myself again once I'd gotten some help."
Jenna

"I started to notice that I didn't feel quite right in the first few weeks, the baby blues had come and gone, but I felt so detached yet overwhelmed. I struggled through till

about nine months postpartum, when it all just got too much and my husband insisted I went to the doctor. I was started on antidepressants, and things improved a little. I still didn't feel great though and I ended up referring myself for some therapy which was really helpful. It took me about a year after going to therapy for me to feel like I'd fully come out of the other side."

Sharon

BUMPS IN THE ROAD

Recovery is not a linear path, and there will be ups and down, along with potential relapses in mental health. Hopefully, whatever support your loved one has engaged in will have taken account of this, and there will be a relapse prevention plan in place. If not, however, it can be helpful to know what the potential setbacks might be, and how they might impact your loved one.

RETURNING TO WORK

Going back to work after maternity leave is a huge adjustment for most new mums, but for a woman who is recovering from PND/PPD the extra load, expectation and juggling can be really difficult to navigate. It can be helpful to plan well in advance for any return to work and build this up slowly to give your loved one (and everyone else) time to adjust. In addition, mum guilt can return with vengeance during this time. Leaving a child distressed at nursery, or not being home in time for dinner, can be very triggering. Keep talking to your loved one and keep reassuring her that while she *feels* guilty, she is *not* guilty for going back to work. It might be helpful for you to think about upping the support during this time of transition, reminding her that she has the tools to cope and knowing that you can help her seek additional support again if required.

HAVING ANOTHER CHILD

Having another child following PND/PPD can be very scary and triggering for all involved. While there is an increased risk of developing PND/PPD with subsequent children, that does not mean that all women will. It is important in subsequent pregnancies that this is proactively assessed and managed. If your loved one goes on to have another baby, it will be important to make the healthcare professionals aware of the fact she experienced PND/PPD previously. This way, extra support, extra check-ins and quick responsiveness to symptoms will be more readily available.

"I experienced PND/PPD after my first daughter. I was worried about getting it again after my second. I was much

more aware second time around, although that didn't stop it from happening. But because I was more aware, and people around me were too, it meant I recognized it earlier and got help quicker. It was still really hard, but easier than the first time."

Olivia

"When I fell pregnant with my second, I was so anxious about everything going wrong again (I also realized I'd experienced some birth trauma first time round which I hadn't really processed). Once my second daughter was born, I actually felt much better, the birth had been lovely; however, around about six months postpartum, I felt my mood deteriorating again. I was getting really irritable with my eldest and so overwhelmed and depressed. I recognized it much sooner this time around and went straight to the doctor and engaged in therapy again. I'm now three years on from that time and I still struggle with my mood from time to time, particularly if the girls are being challenging, but I know how to manage it better now."

Sharon

The most important thing when it comes to setbacks is reminding yourself and your loved one that it is OK. We are all human, and the stresses and pressures of life can get to us.

Finding things hard or experiencing a relapse only makes us human, and is certainly not evidence of failure. Seeing these setbacks as normal takes the shame and guilt out of them, and allows your loved one to access support quickly.

So while recovery is very much possible, bearing in mind that it is not straightforward, quick, all or nothing and linear will help both you and your loved one manage your expectations. It will also help you recognize when a little more support is needed without the panic or shame that things have 'gone back the way they were'. But the most important thing to remember is that recovery, in whatever shape, is possible and your loved one can get to a place of wellness, and get to enjoy motherhood.

FINAL WORDS

I hope this book has provided you with some understanding of what your loved one might be experiencing, as well as empowering you and equipping you with the tools and information to be able to support her in her recovery. Providing this support is no small task, and one that is fuelled with worry and frustration. The most important message I want you to take away from this book is that you do not have to do it alone. There is help and support out there for your loved one, but also for you. Seek that support out sooner rather than later.

Remember, your loved one can get better. She can feel better and can recover from this dark place she is in. There is hope, and with a better understanding of her difficulties, as well as an idea of how you and others can help, she will get to a place of recovery and will begin enjoying motherhood as she has so deserved.

Thank you for choosing this book, and please do share it with anyone else who might find it beneficial! The more we know and talk about these issues, the less shame and guilt a mother might experience, and the quicker we can support her in her motherhood journey.

ACKNOWLEDGEMENTS

I would like to thank my husband, David, for showing me unrelentless support and belief – he could probably have done with this book in our early years of parenting. And my darling daughters who, despite those rocky first couple of years in the depths of PND/PPD, have shown me the joy of motherhood and inspire all that I do. And to my amazing family and friends, who when I have had little belief in myself, have shown me theirs in abundance – and held me accountable when procrastination hit!

I also want to thank my wonderful Instagram community, from whom I have been gifted insight and real-life experience. Their willingness and generosity to offer their words and stories to be included in this book has been a real gift. They are brave and courageous women and men, who are speaking out and normalizing maternal mental health difficulties.

I would also like to thank Welbeck Balance for pushing me out of my comfort zone and being patient with me while writing a book during the most challenging year I could have imagined.

Finally, I would like to thank every one of my clients. It is an honour and privilege to be invited into your world and be given the trust to support and empower you in your therapeutic journey. I learn and grow daily through our work, each one of you inspires me to push myself as I watch you push yourselves. I feel truly grateful to be able to do the job that I do!

REFERENCES

1. de Cock, ESA, Henrichs, J, Klimstra, TA et al (2017). Longitudinal Associations Between Parental Bonding, Parenting Stress, and Executive Functioning in Toddlerhood. *J Child Fam Stud*, 26, pp. 1723-1733. Available at: doi.org/10.1007/s10826-017-0679-7 [Accessed 6 July 2021].

2. Fuchs, A, Möhler, E, Reck, C, Resch, F and Kaess, M (2016). The Early Mother-to-Child Bond and Its Unique Prospective Contribution to Child Behavior Evaluated by Mothers and Teachers. *Psychopatholgy*, 49, pp. 211-216. Available at: dx.doi.org/10.1159%2F000445439 [Accessed 13 July 2021].

3. Kendrick, KM (2000). Oxytocin, Motherhood and Bonding. *Experimental Physiology*, 85, pp. 111-124. Available at: physoc.onlinelibrary.wiley.com/doi/pdf/10.1111/j.1469-445X.2000.tb00014.x [Accessed 6 July 2021].

4. NICE (2009). *Depression in Adults: Recognition and Management (CG90)*. Available at: www.nice.org.uk/guidance/cg90/resources/depression-in-adults-recognition-and-management-pdf-975742636741 [PDF accessed 6 July 2021].

5. Rasmussen, MHL et al (2017). Risk, Treatment Duration, and Recurrence Risk of Postpartum Affective Disorder in Women with no Prior Psychiatric History: A Population-based Cohort Study. *PLOS Medicine*. Available at: https://journals.plos.org/plosmedicine/article?id=10.1371/journal.pmed.1002392 [Accessed 6 July 2021].

6. Tseng, J, Poppenk, J (2020). Brain Meta-state Transitions Demarcate Thoughts Across Task Contexts Exposing the Mental Noise of Trait Neuroticism. *Nat Commun* 11, p. 3480. Available at: doi.org/10.1038/s41467-020-17255-9 [Accessed 6 July 2021].

7. VanderKruik R et al (2017). The Global Prevalence of Postpartum Psychosis: A Systematic Review. *BMC Psychiatry*, 17, p. 272. Available at: www.ncbi.nlm.nih.gov/pmc/articles/PMC5534064/ [Accessed 13 July 2021].

8. Winston, R and Chicot, R (2016). The Importance of Early Bonding on the Long-term Mental Health and Resilience of Children. *London Journal of Primary Care*, 8(1), pp. 12-14. Available at: doi.org/10.1080/17571472.2015.1133012 [Accessed 6 July 2021].

9. Wisner K, Sit DKY, McShea MC, Rizzo DM, Zoretich RA, Hughes CL et al (2013). Onset Timing, Thoughts of Self-harm, and Diagnoses in Postpartum Women with Screen-positive Depression Findings. *JAMA Psychiatry*; 70, pp. 490-498.

USEFUL RESOURCES

The following websites provide information specific to PND/PPD.

- APNI – Association for Post Natal Illness: apni.org
- PANDAS – PND Awareness and Support: pandasfoundation.org.uk
- PSI – Postpartum Support International: www.postpartum.net
- Fourth Trimester Project: newmomhealth.com

The following websites provide general information on depression, with content relating to PND/PPD.

- Mind UK: www.mind.org.uk
- Mental Health America: www.mhanational.org
- National Alliance on Mental Illness (NAMI): www.nami.org
- Canadian Mental Health Association: cmha.ca
- Beyond Blue: www.beyondblue.org.au
- Head to Health: headtohealth.gov.au
- Mental Health Australia: mhaustralia.org

- Mental Health Foundation of New Zealand: www.mentalhealth.org.nz
- SANE Australia: www.sane.org

Information on Medication and Breastfeeding

- La Leche League International: www.llli.org
- Kelly Mom: kellymom.com
- Breastfeeding Network UK: www.breastfeedingnetwork.org.uk

Recommended Reading

Cree, M (2015). *The Compassionate Mind Approach to Postnatal Depression: Using Compassion Focused Therapy to Enhance Mood, Confidence and Bonding.* Robinson.

Hanzack, E (1998). *Eyes Without Sparkle: A Journey Through Postnatal Illness.* Routledge.

Jolin, L (2019). *Coping with Birth Trauma and Postnatal Depression.* Sheldon Press.

Kleiman, K (2013). *This Isn't What I expected: Overcoming Postpartum Depression.* Da Capo.

Spencer, O (2014). *Sad Dad: An Exploration of Postnatal Depression in Fathers.* Free Association Books.

Wheatley, S (2006). *Coping with Postnatal Depression.* Sheldon Press.

TriggerHub.org is one of the most elite and scientifically proven forms of mental health intervention

Trigger Publishing is the leading independent mental health and wellbeing publisher in the UK and US. Clinical and scientific research conducted by assistant professor Dr Kristin Kosyluk and her highly acclaimed team in the Department of Mental Health Law & Policy at the University of South Florida (USF), as well as complementary research by her peers across the US, has independently verified the power of lived experience as a core component in achieving mental health prosperity. Specifically, the lived experiences contained within our bibliotherapeutic books are intrinsic elements in reducing stigma, making those with poor mental health feel less alone, providing the privacy they need to heal, ensuring they know the essential steps to kick-start their own journeys to recovery, and providing hope and inspiration when they need it most.

Delivered through TriggerHub, our unique online portal and accompanying smartphone app, we make our library of bibliotherapeutic titles and other vital resources accessible to individuals and organizations anywhere, at any time and with complete privacy, a crucial element of recovery. As such, TriggerHub is the primary recommendation across the UK and US for the delivery of lived experiences.

At Trigger Publishing and TriggerHub, we proudly lead the way in making the unseen become seen. We are dedicated to humanizing mental health, breaking stigma and challenging outdated societal values to create real action and impact. Find out more about our world-leading work with lived experience and bibliotherapy via triggerhub.org, or by joining us on:

🐦 @triggerhub_

ⓕ @triggerhub.org

📷 @triggerhub_

Printed in the USA
CPSIA information can be obtained
at www.ICGtesting.com
JSHW011423230224
57889JS00029B/56